FOR WARNED
ATTENTION READERS OF THIS BOOK

F.Y.I.—For your information—this book contains some adult language. It is a most common language, learned in America and spoken by millions of Americans, both Blacks and Whites, young and old, and the rich and poor! I, the author, have chosen the language within – to emphasize the importance of the thoughts shared, and to reach as many people as possible with the truth!

If you are offended by popular vulgar-terms of contemporary speech, or are uncomfortable with harsh or crude language, then you have my permission to politely put my book down, and go and purchase another one containing a less truthful, less passionate tone.

It is an established fact that "*truth*" as it is experienced in it's many artistic and creative venues, can and often times offend some people's sensibilities or taste. My honest intent is not to offend—but to reach and continue to teach "*truth*". So if you feel you can't handle anything more than that which you're already comfortable with, then you might as well call Dr. Jack Kervorkian, and prepare to commit suicide, because life, truth, and our America will tear you a new-ass-hole (especially if you are black), whether you're ready for it or not, comfortable or uncomfortable, blue-collar or white-collar—sooner or later! If you continue to live and move in this world, one day it will happen! Again, especially if you are black.

So the hell with condemning the work just to discredit the author! Let us journey forward and read and review what has been written, to discover what we may "*have in common*"—due to our shared blackness... OK? Someday you (the reader) may come to see and appreciate – just what a great black-psychic I really am, as well as a great contemporary black bard. Look it up!

Enough said – let's get this good shit on the road – I'll drive!...

The Author—Big Brother
Earl Roberts

I Beg Your Damn Pardon—Was It Something I Said?

The Poetic Prose and Unchained Thoughts of a Contemporary Black Man

By
Big Brother
Earl Roberts

B.B.E.R

Canadian Cataloguing in Publication Data

Roberts, Earl.
I beg your damn pardon was it something I said

ISBN 1-55212-353-7

I. Title.
PS3535.O15I2 2000 818'.607 C00-910319-8

TRAFFORD

This book was published on-demand in cooperation with Trafford Publishing.
On-demand publishing is a unique process and service of making a book available for retail sale to the public taking advantage of on-demand manufacturing and Internet marketing.
On-demand publishing includes promotions, retail sales, manufacturing, order fulfilment, accounting and collecting royalties on behalf of the author.

Suite 6E, 2333 Government St., Victoria, B.C. V8T 4P4, CANADA
Phone 250-383-6864 Toll-free 1-888-232-4444 (Canada & US)
Fax 250-383-6804 E-mail sales@trafford.com
Web site www.trafford.com trafford publishing is a division of trafford holdings ltd.
Trafford Catalogue #00-0017 www.trafford.com/robots/00-0017.html

10 9 8 7 6 5 4 3

I BEG YOUR DAMN PARDON!
-WAS IT SOMETHING I SAID?
IS DEDICATED TO A BLACKMAN I NEVER KNEW
BUT WISH I DID

This book of urban prose and unchained black thoughts is dedicated to the black (retired) Marine, who was recently decapitated, dosed with gasoline, and set on fire—out on a lonely road in the great state of Virginia. Not far from a trailer-home, where earlier he had been partying with four white friends, who had also been drinking moonshine, smoking dope, and dropping tranquilizers, and who later were charged with their black "*friend's*" murder … .no, this brother did nothing to provoke them!

It happened in July—in The Year of Our Lord 1997, and from varied published accounts, black people across the nation saw no need to do, or demand a damn thing—while the local white sheriff shouted out to the world that "*race had nothing to do with this heinous crime.*" I know this recently deceased human-being's name, and I shall remember it, his sacrifice, his service to his country, and most of all his blind trust in his friends! I will shout his name out to the world! If you to want to know and honor his name, well damn it!—Look it up under the heading "America Home of The Brave and The Free", except in Virginia, if you're black with white friends! Better watch where you party cause you don't want to be anywhere in America—where you are in the minority, and someone white is serving you drugs and home-made whiskey! … Pray with me here!

"*May God have mercy on us all*"—or at least make it possible for all responsible black people in American to afford a damn shot-gun or automatic rifle (like most white people have now-a-days!)—before it's to late for us! Oh Lord—why can't my people remember, "*diamonds come from little bits and pieces of black-coal, under great continuous pressure, and a black person's life is as valuable as any other*"… especially our brother, Mr. Garnett Johnson … He trusted white-folks, he thought they were his "*Friends*!"

As it is written herein—so be it black
Because Black is Beautiful and I pray forever
Big Brother Earl Roberts

ONWARD AND UPWARD
LET'S GET THIS PARTY STARTED

"We younger Negro/black artist who create, now intend to express our individual dark-skinned selves without fear or shame. If the white folks are pleased, we are glad. If they are not, it doesn't matter. We know we are beautiful and ugly too. The Tom-Tom cries and the Tom-Tom laughs. If negro/black people are pleased, we are glad. If they are not, their displeasure doesn't matter either. We build our temples for tomorrow, strong as we know how, and we stand on top of the mountain of true freedom—within ourselves."

Langston Hughes

"Thank you Brother Hughes May I inspire others as you have inspired me."

When I am no longer available to physically touch, and my spirit soars upon the wings of heavenly bliss—don't put anything on my grave marker but what you've read above. Anything else and I promise to return to haunt your black-asses … .*"Am I serious? … . Ya'll better go ask somebody!"*—read me and believe me!

"I Don't Play!" Big Brother Earl Roberts

I Beg Your Damn Pardon—
Was I Something I Said?

CONTENTS

THE LASTQUESTION OF BLACK ON BLACK CRIME

ALEXANDER THE GREAT (DESTROYER)
NAPOLEON THE GREAT (DESTROYER)
THE ROMAN EMPIRE (KILLERS)
CAESAR NERO (KILLER)
THE OLD CATHOLIC CHURCH
WORLD WAR ONE
WORLD WAR TWO
THE ATOMIC BOMB
ADOLF HITLER AND THE THIRD REICH
THE JEWISH HOLOCAUST
JACK THE RIPPER
THE CONQUEST OF AFRICA
THE KOREAN CONFLICT
THE BLACK HOLOCAUST (1600—?)
THE VIETNAM WAR
THE BOSTON STRANGLER
THE BOLEO, OKLAHOMA LAND GRAB
ROSEWOOD, FLORIDA SLAUGHTER
THE AMERICAN INDIAN SLAUGHTERS
THE TUSKEEGEE EXPERIMENT
JIM CROW SEGREGATION/LYNCHINGS
THE ROSEWOOD, TEXAS SLAUGHTER
JOHN WAYNE GASEY (MONSTER)
TED THE TERRIBLE BUNDY (KILLER)
CHARLES MANSON (MONSTER)
SON OF SAM (KILLER)
THE HILL-SIDE STRANGLER (KILLER)
JUAN CARLOS (MONSTER)
LA COSTRA-NOSTRA (MAFIA KILLERS)
OLIVER NORTH (D&D)
THE C.I.A. (D.D. & D.)
THE F.B.I. (HIT SQUADS)

JOHN THE MOB GOTTI
IVAN THE GREEDY BOSKEY
JEFFREY DAHMER (MONSTER)
MICHAEL RIPP-OFF MILKEN
THE ARYAN NATION
THE KU-KLUX-KLAN (1800-199?)
MARK FURHMAN
L.A. EX. P.C. DARRYL GATES
EX. PRES. R. NIXONE
X. PRES. R. RAY-GUN
DENNY MCCLAIN
THE UNI-BOMBER/DESERT STORM
TIMOTHY MCVEIGH
THE MILITIA MOVEMENT
EX. PRES. G. BUSH AND SON NEIL
N.Y.P.D.'S 70TH PRECT, PLUNGER

Moreover, many, many more white names and evil events—both past and present, should go on this list! A truly serious question begs to be asked of my people—black people! Should we be truly concerned about black-on-black crime? Shit, compared to what? Black people need to stop today (right now), from believing all the bullshit hype! Absolutely nobody the world over destroys life and property-bigger and better than white people! (the proof is in their history). Black Americans had better unite real soon—before the headlines read: Race war erupts on American soil—young blacks violating curfews and U.S. restrictions, ordered shot on sight!—President and whites are dumbfounded! Could this happen here? Start from the top, add your own names and events, then answer truthfully—Yes! It could! Believe it! Will blacks be prepared? After more painful lessons at the hands of racist-violent, white Americans, maybe we'll be forced to reunite as a race, as a shocked and finally convinced survivors group of domesticated slaves, or incarcerated sharecroppers—after the war! Black on black crime is indeed fallacious! Black unity- a must—for our future survival depends on it!

WHITE AMERICA—WILL YOU EVER UNDERSTAND?

White America, will you ever understand? What it truly means to be black in America, and still feel like you're living in a foreign land?

White America, will you ever understand? Why it's so frustrating for millions of hardworking black women and black men in a capitalistic land?

White America, will you ever truly come to know? If you only read the dailies and watch the evening news—no! Why for so many blacks, anger and frustration is all they can show?

White America, You won't ever know what it means to be black, desiring to be accepted as an American, and constantly being told to "*stand back*"- until millions of you change places in this great experiment gone wrong, with millions wearing black faces, who may have stayed in this country way too long.

White America, will you ever understand? I doubt it! Your racism runs so deep! Keep praying white America, for millions of black Americans to remain mentally asleep!

I WONDER AS I PONDER WHY?

Millions of white Americans are arming themselves (heavily) each and every year. I read a book once entitled: Two Americas One White/One Black—Separate and Unequal. I wonder as I ponder—why? Black people aren't doing the same.

Will America's armed forces (within the military/both blacks and whites) come to the defense of black people's neighborhood borders? I wonder whose side they'll be on—against the white racist armed and trained militias like it does for its allies around the world? I wonder as I ponder—why?

Black people drive and own new cars almost at twice the rate of most middle-class folks in this country, yet they don't own one automobile company or auto assembly plant. I wonder as I ponder—why? Are blacks being taken for a one-way ride?

Most white Americans are willing to risk skin cancer (and even death) just to wear a bronze, or deep, dark tan, year round if possible. You know—I wonder as I ponder—why? They still refuse to accept us as equals, those born that way.

White businesses and especially Madison Avenue ad agencies got their hooks (teeth, hands, and feet) into the pockets of black people so deeply, that our young brothers and sisters can't keep their trousers up off their asses ... I wonder as I ponder—why?

They constantly brag that they can sell sand to a black man living on a desert, and today it's natural spring water, to black people who just happen to be surrounded by three oceans and several seas, so again, I wonder as I ponder—why? Drinking water isn't free anymore.

Enough already! What is this scientific evidence that the FDA and Department of Agriculture claims to have that shows "*soul food*" is dangerous to our health and may cause cancer—bullshit! I wonder as I ponder—why? My momma's "*chittlings*" taste so damn good, and my white co-workers keep begging for the recipe! Oh HELL yes, I wonder as I ponder why? Don't you? Maybe you should!

SLOW THIS GODDAMN WORLD DOWN, I THINK I WANT TO GET OFF!

Oh God, awoke again this morning, and turned on T.V. hoping beyond hope to be greeted by some positive world news for a change… big mistake! All over the country (it seemed like all over the world) white males are screaming about reverse discrimination, and filing reverse discrimination charges. At first I said, Oh shit, what the hell is old Mister Charlie up to now? Every time I think I've got white folks figured out, they get creative and toss me a serious curve (and the rest of black America too, I surmise). White people are just so ingenious aren't they? With their divide and conquer racial strategy! Talk about an affirmative-action backlash! Check this shit out—*"they're evil, demanding, untrustworthy, deadly, still inferior savages, who complain constantly about the system lately, all the while asking for special treatment, quotas, and lowered standards."*

Word for word off the telly, as spoken by a white southern college student recently. So answer this question black America: who is it that still speaks and thinks like this? (hint-white folks) *What is the best way for us to protect ourselves and our families from these lazy undeserving creatures? The best way is to sue them all and any company or university that continues to practice affirmative-action. Yeah, that's the ticket, just sue the bastards for "reverse discrimination".* Then again, white leaders are very seldom at a loss for creative solutions to thwart the successful progress of black folks are they? Let's see, how about trying—#1—Lock them all up. Incarcerate as many of them as possible in jails and prisons, keeping them uneducated and unrehabilitated at the same time, and farm their labor out without due compensation so that they won't be a total drain on the system, or, #2—Keep them and their kind isolated and confined in specific black zip-coded urban areas and encourage them to spend their money outside of these areas, so they'll be easier to monitor and control when needed, or, #3—Start another war. Then send as many as possible off to fight it, where many will get killed, protecting someone else's freedom and rights, and the few that return home will be so messed up they won't be able to hold down a job or compete successfully for a college grant or scholarships, because they'll be too high to read the damn things, after becoming hooked on foreign drugs and learned violent behavior, or #4—Better yet, let's just flood their communities with a new deadly drug (crack) and hundreds of cheap automatic weapons, then encourage them a little (with blood-money) to kill themselves off so the blame for their self-destruction will rest solely on their black-ass shoulders.

How about all of the above solutions, or maybe a potent mix or a combination of these tactics and several others we're planning. White folks for sure are presently searching for a new and insidious game plan to combat their perceived problems and self created fears of too many blacks becoming successful (if not equal) and prosperous. Specifically due to "*affirmative-action*" and other social-civil mandated programs created during the late 60's and 70's to redress past wrongs by white America and insure equality of opportunity for black Americans. The real problem we seem to have here, is that these programs and affirmative-action have been way too successful and too quick to work over the past 30 years. Sounds familiar? It should. It's still happening all over America. Know this my people; if these racist tactics and solutions were aimed at white Americans by black governmental leaders (or a black uncontrollable president, if ever), it would have resulted in white America declaring war on all of us, and black people being stripped of their citizenship, and shipped lock-stock-and-barrel back to mother Africa, quick, fast and in a hurry, at no charge to any of us!

Affirmative-action backlash? Sure, if we continue to allow white leaders and some of our own (like his Honor Clown Thomas) to get away with this truly evil, ingenious, treachery? If black folks stand idly by and allow this to happen, then we should prepare to watch the real black fall-out from an all too real younger black American back-lash! Warning: Today it's California's Formula 209, tomorrow, it'll be the U.S. Bill-of-Rights Amendment #409 (my prediction). The amendment's (409) content—"*spray gasoline on all the black faces, after building massive ovens, herd them into same, turn up the heat, (which is already on) and then strike a match, burn for a couple of days, then just wipe the ovens clean, which will automatically wipe clean the white collective consciousness of greed, fear, and deep racial hatred*" (it could happen).

Question of my people: Did any of you who sit at home all day in front of the television set always waiting for some courageous, strong, and intelligent black person to come along to fight your racial battles, hear this on the evening news today? "*California and Texas*" universities and one in Michigan are burning down, burning real bad, not from massive body-ovens, they're burning from the effects of Proposal 209, no more affirmative action or quotas on our campuses, damn! From Harper's Index, the percentage of change in black students admitted to Berkley's Law School since California banned affirmative action last year (of those who qualified), but refused/chose not to attend was only 14, down from 156 the year before! We don't want to know what happened (the loss) between 96 and 97s enrollment over at California's medical college do we? No, I didn't think so, we don't want to light any fuses that are determined to stay un-lit? Shit! I say "*burn-baby-burn*!" Fuck it! We have fought too hard and long to come this far to allow white racist conservatives to send us and our children back towards plantations "*Burn Baby Burn*!" Violence for the sake of violence—is impracticable and immoral. "*Violence in the cause of self-defense is intelligence*"—Malcolm X. Vote to save affirmative action! What's next?

By the way my people—In 1996, the Federal Affirmative Action set aside policy of the U.S. small business administration was changed to exclude black folks and replaced them with preferences for Indians and white women. The current racist trend of "*work-fare*" replacing welfare around the country focuses on finding jobs and job training for women (both black and white), but once again, avoids the issue of educating or training out of work or out of school young black males! Smell a conspiracy here! I do and so should you, damn it!

NO THANK YOU WHITE FOLKS

What the hell is it now white folks? Everyday it's something new with you! An apology for slavery? Naah! it's much too late! Reparations for all black Americans like those you gave to Japanese-Americans? Naah—just wouldn't work! Why not? Well, you wouldn't want the whole world to see White people themselves coming out of the racial-closets, suddenly professing that their great-grandmothers (and great-grandfathers) were part black, or a slave, or black mistress/nanny in some slave-master's house, (it's called miscegenation) and many would be able to prove it! Therefore, they too would be entitled to monetary compensation, especially if blacks today were gonna receive any! Isn't this why white folks didn't deliver on their documented promise to supply every adult freed slave with at least 40-acres and a healthy mule? Even then they didn't intend to share America's wealth-just to control it for themselves! A U.S. apology—what's the point? United States cash reparations to the ancestors of ex-slaves—no thanks. <u>Way too many white folks will be getting in line</u>! Damn! How many times must black folk be reminded, "*beware of Greeks bearing gifts—like a Trojan horse.*"

BLACK VIETNAM

On the wall of the Vietnam War Memorial in Washington, D.C. there are listed 7,241 names of African-Americans who died for this country in Vietnam, don't believe it! 7,241 equals only 12.4% of all the names on the wall. A total of 998,000 blacks truly served in this war, with over half in the infantry and support services, and at least half of those were forced to serve out on the front lines. Ok, you do the math. Maybe they need a bigger wall in D.C., or maybe our black vets need their own memorial. America has always had a problem getting our numbers right—during peace time (the census), and even in fighting America's war (body counts). Even so, we (the black majority) continue to serve her and obey her laws. Personally, I wonder how many black bodies, or black Vietnamese war babies were abandoned (left behind) by America in '72. I wonder what those colored rice-growers truly feel today about America's black warriors, who served in Vietnam so courageously and valiantly, then came home and couldn't get a job, but could get high off American drugs... jobs they were told were scarce, but dope was not! ... and the beat goes on... Damn! The movie "*Dead Presidents*" told only half the story, the other half has been classified by the U.S. Military as "*top secret*".

JEWS ADVERTISE THEIR PAIN

Oh them Jewish people. What a smart people they are. Why is it in all the nation's media, at some point and time, every so often, in our recent history (the last 40-50 years past) and even into our near future I suspect (40-50 years to come), we constantly continue to hear about a Jewish "holocaust" (the thorough destruction of a people, especially by fire), or about Adolph Hitler and the Nazis planned death and destruction of 6-10 million Jews. Just how many more news clips or commentaries must we endure about the National Jewish Holocaust Museum located in our country's capital city? It's construction, financing, purpose, it's frightening artifacts and solemn historical displays. Please America, give me a break! In all the media, print, radio, T.V., and now on my computer, Jewish leaders are constantly reminding all of us of their collective past pain and suffering. Well, enough already! I would truly like to hear, read, see, touch and feel more facts concerning the black holocaust.

Remembering where and when 50-60 million black people were captured, stolen, chained, shipped, beat, killed and maimed, thrown overboard slaughtered by the thousands, castrated, brainwashed, starved, repeatedly raped, re-enslaved, bought and sold like cattle, whipped and branded, lied to, denied freedom, denied access to education and the right to vote, forcibly taught to hate and despise themselves but not others, cheated out of their savings, land and meager possessions, over worked, under paid, burned and lynched. First not allowed to—then later encouraged to practice a foreign religion, separated and segregated, intentionally divided (especially their families), labeled, stereotyped, disrespected and treated as inferior, constantly insulted and discriminated against, last hired-first fired, falsely arrested and often incarcerated and rewarded handsomely for selling out and snitching on their own people (meritorious manumission). Let us not forget the continued overt and racially motivated assassination of our great black leaders, time and time again. Over and over again! Shall I go on?

There is more, and still in a black-ass majority city like that of Detroit, Michigan, a city with the world's biggest and best monument to black people and their great black historical culture (the newly built Museum of Afro-American History), less than 400,000 blacks have crossed it's Afro-centric threshold while a million more live nearby. How utterly sad! While more than five states with large black populations within them, are less than a 10-hour drive away! Yes, I've personally read, heard, seen (as was so dramatically displayed in the movie Roots), touched and felt, and remembered our black holocaust, and to tell you all the painful truth, my soul will never forget it; nor should the soul of America, especially black Americans!

Question to my people: Will your souls ever forget <u>our</u> black holocaust? Damn it, have they (your souls) forgotten already? Maybe black people can learn something about <u>remembering</u> an evil and painful history from the Jewish people and their continuing self-sponsoring (I am truly convinced they don't want to see another Hitler), self-paid-for Holocaust ad campaign? Maybe not! Maybe it's our own "*black-ass destiny*" to forget the evil middle-passage, and our pain-filled history of slavery and post-slavery years here in America. Maybe we <u>world-community negroes</u> are destined to become once again—an invisible people, or will we continue to debate with one another the merits or demerits of continuing to advertise our own pain with the hope that by the time we decide to pool our financial resources or not, advertising may not be necessary! <u>Wanna bet me what the Jews will be doing 100 years hence</u>? Oh, come on! Please bet me a few of those sweet black-asses, cause lately true black asses (the blacker the berry, the sweeter the juice) have been mighty hard to find. I'll keep looking. In the mean time, you can love me or hate me, but-cha will respect me. I vote to continue to advertise! I wasn't born to be invisible! And neither were our ancestors (our roots), who should never be allowed to become invisible to the world, and especially to our own black youth! Let us commit our dollars and time to advertising black Americans "collective pain and suffering" in America! Even today, black people's lack of economical and political cohesiveness and dis-unity has always left us vulnerable to control and abuse by others. Jews don't have this problem!

AN AMERICAN INDIAN MESSAGE

In 1973, the Menominee Indians won back their right to be and remain an Indian Nation-within-a-nation (U.S.A.), and to keep their lands and tribal government sovereign unto themselves. Sometime in 2001, our government will try again to steal their lumber-rich lands and timber businesses and thereby steal their cultural base and self-identity! I say, fight on brother red-man, fight the holy fight when the time comes! There is no greater glory than to die fighting for the control of your own destiny, and the future destiny of your tribe and it's culture. You, my red brothers, have many sympathizers in the black communities of the black tribes in America. Stand fast, red man, be ever vigilant and ready! Your struggle, like our own in America, is not over yet, not by far. Keep in mind, it is much more heroic to live ten minutes standing and facing one's enemies, than to kneel down for life just to die a coward. My Indian brothers, did you know America's military has the gall to call the loss of a nuclear bomber a "*broken arrow*?" What would you call the total loss of your present day lands and remaining culture at the hands of today's pale faces? Call it genetic annihilation. Our world would not be complete without your people in it! The great universal spirit will watch over and guide your race in the trying and dangerous days ahead, I'm sure. Peace! Never say die- never surrender! Remember my native American brothers—what Oglala Chief Luther Standing Bear in November, 98's national geographic said (p.19).—"*Most American Indians do not think of the open plans, the beautiful rolling hills, the multi-named trees of the forest, and winding streams... as wild. Only to the white man is nature a wilderness.*" Your trees are living things and give you life—fight for them! Peace, my colored brothers—peace until...

ODE TO SECRETARY OF COMMERCE, RON BROWN (RECENTLY DECEASED) IN HONOR OF YOUR LIFE OF SERVICE—YOUR GREATNESS

Oh America, oh America, can you hear the cries, the shouts, the screams— a great country in itself, a great force for good or great evil. Can you hear the people, their constant pleas for more mercy, more love, more openness, and more honesty — the very virtues of the saints and saviors. Is it not so true, that when great men of a great country begin to die under any natural or unnatural circumstances, so shall that great country become not so great... and over time, less than it could become, if great men were allowed to live.

Black America, a serious question lingers upon my mind, of how and why another great black man becomes lost to us, becoming lost in time, time and time again. Why, at the very pinnacle of his career and successful life! If this man is a black man, highly intelligent, or highly educated, whose usually embattled with some form of suffering and strife, (internally if not externally shown) against a racist society that's forever suspicious of his position of power or wealth simply because of the color of his skin. A color other than a white-pale face. Must he be subjected to elimination or racist vilification!

I'd like to ask someone in Washington, what or who was truly behind the untimely demise of our brother Secretary of Commerce of the United States of America, Mr. Ron Brown? Why is it that it appears (at least to me), that far too many intelligent and incorruptible black men in this country and around the world are perceived of as some kind of threat to the white-ruling elite in this country and around the world, in white controlled areas? Why are powerful and successful black men viewed as a serious threat to their power or positions of wealth, even to their physical health and well being? A threat so compelling as to warrant their nullification or elimination from the face of the earth. At whatever cost, often under covert and mysterious circumstances? Am I the only one to ask this question of Uncle

Sam and white America? Will there be an honest answer forthcoming anytime soon? I doubt it.

I'd like to ask someone in Washington, just what was the real nature and depth of the political and friendship relationships of our current President and Secretary of Commerce, Mr. Brown? I'd like it to be made just a little clearer to me, and other deeply concerned blacks, why Mr. Brown would be subpoenaed to appear before a select-investigative committee looking into the president's political and personal dealings (operations and actions) of the Whitehouse proper? Also, again, just what were the allegations and/or circumstances that led up to Mr. Ron Brown's office and personal life being scrutinized and investigated so deeply? The media reported something about possible bribe-taking or influence peddling by the Secretary here in this country and abroad. None of which was ever proven, I recall. Am I the only one to ask this question, and expect an answer from Washington? I doubt it.

I'd like to ask someone in Washington, Just what did Mr. Ron Brown's post-presidential meeting entail, prior to his ill-fated departure abroad? Just a couple of weeks before he was schedule to testify before a Senate select-committee or Grand Jury looking into the White House's possible involvement in a cover up in the Whitewater scandal (on-going investigation), and concerns of possible campaign finances irregularities (another on-going investigation) for violations involving high-ranking White House officials. Indeed, allegedly involving the President, his wife and the Vice-President. I wonder as do many others I'm sure, what might have presidential friend and attorney Mr. Vance Foster known about any Whitewater cover-up, or Travel-Gate that may have contributed to his (untimely) suicide? Wasn't he, as it was reported, also friends with the Secretary as well as the President for sometime past? Any honest answer from Washington, anytime soon? I doubt it.

I'd like to ask someone in Washington, just what Mr. Ron Brown may have said to the President at their last meeting, regarding his up-coming testimony that may have changed the very nature of their long-term friendship (since the glory days back in Arkansas) when our President was Governor of that great southern slave state. I can't help wondering if conversation came up as to the possible, or probable testimony of Mr. Brown's (or what might have been said to the Secretary by the president) upon his return trip from Croatia regarding possible questions that may be put to him by special prosecutor Ken Starr at those hearings he was scheduled to attend after his mission abroad? Did Mr. Brown tell the President that he desired Presidential protection if the committee's heat became too hot for him to handle alone, or was he just naive about trusting white folks?! Would Washington answer, I seriously doubt it!

I would like to ask someone in Washington, if anyone may have overheard an order being given to someone from the dirty-operations department. within or near the White House (unbeknown to the President, of course) to make absolutely sure that the Secretary's plane not make it back to the shores of the United States of America?! To prevent any further worry, or testimony, or loose-ends, regarding the President's wheelings and dealings, both past and present? Would Washington tell us the truth if asked at this late date? I doubt it!

I would like to ask someone in Washington about several mysterious and (today) unverifiable allegations surrounding the crash of Secretary Brown's plane. I would ask them about the pilot, was he not the Air Force's best? What of the discrepancies regarding the weather between the print media and that of television on that fateful day? One reporting severe inclement weather while the other reported minor rain and fog? What of the fact that two of the three planes on Mr. Brown's journey, landed safely just prior to his plane's final approach to the same airstrip (air-field with plenty of lights and radar beacons) located in the mountains!? And what of the rumor that there was one female survivor of the crash, who was miraculously still alive and conscious and only slightly injured, having mysteriously died within one mile of medical facilities by helicopter!? Would Washington confirm or deny these die-hard rumors/questions, I doubt it!

I would like to ask someone in Washington, just what the hell was done (if anything) by our contemporary Black

Caucus Congressional members put in office to ensure and protect their congressional districts and their black voting constituents? What questions were asked, if any, by them of the White House proper, that would validate or not, the White House's interpretation and subsequent investigation, and later reports to the media of the accident scene and events leading up to and culminating in the so-called accidental death of our Secretary of Commerce and his entire entourage, flying with him on this ill-fated, yet memorable day? What could someone in the Black Caucus tell us, maybe the truth, I seriously doubt it!

I would like to ask someone in Washington, anyone within or near the White House, if they've heard of a traditional (political good-ole-boy's joke) governmental legacy/conspiracy by either the Illumanati or wealthy-white W.A.S.P. of this country to keep the White House predominantly white as well as the three branches of our government, (the Supreme Court, the Senate, the Congress) for as long as possible, by any means necessary! Would someone out in Washington, D.C. please tell me, if there is any truth to the past rumors that the Kennedys were planning (had secretly talked about) putting the Rev. Martin Luther King on the Democratic ticket to run with Robert Kennedy as Vice President of this great country back in 1968? Just prior to their deaths under mysterious circumstances? What about those mysterious and threatening phone calls to a past presidential black hopeful, the Rev. Jessie Jackson back in the early days of his Rainbow Coalition, that allegedly told him or someone in his family he'd better refuse the nomination if offered to him by the Democratic party at that time, or he would never be around to see his kids graduate from college! Even more recently we should recall, a televised interview with our black Desert Storm victorious Commander-in-Chief, Gen. Colin Power and his wife, where she was asked on a live TV interview if she had any desire to see her husband run for the highest office in the land. Where she immediately responded, *"No, I'm extremely concerned for Colin's health and safety, and he knows this. I don't want him to run for President, period."*

So for just one last time, I'd like to ask someone in Washington, was there the slightest possibility that a black man had once again gained too much power and insider knowledge, in becoming Secretary of Commerce of the United States, and a black (I mean light-skinned) power threat to the white-ruling class burguiouse of America? Did that other party of the wealth-elephant-class elite feel threatened by the opened friendship of a powerful and handsome black man and a powerful some say handsome white Vice President, maybe sharing a desk in the future of the White House? Surely the Oval Office would become tainted in some racist way, if it hadn't become so already with all the black traffic passing through its hallowed doors in recent years. All of these great contemporary black men (some dead, some still alive and vulnerable) seem to me, a free-thinking and intelligent black observer, to have had several things in common. #1-The obvious visible genetic marker (that just won't be faded) of color, or being of black descent (even if one or two of them didn't think so). #2-They all held prior positions of high public-esteem, with some power or influence over a large segment of the black-voting-public. #3-They each was well respected and liked by millions of blacks and whites—liberals alike all around the country. Question to my people, how many of us truly believe that old Mr. Charlie (Old Uncle Sam or some of his rich-racist nephews) may be truly guilty of a racial/political/wealthy—W.A.S.P. (or Catholic) conspiracy—to keep the white-house pure and white in this country forever! Will we ever have a black Vice-President or black President in this great melting pot of ours? I would like to ask someone in Washington this very question, but I'll pass—because I doubt it will ever happen!

It has been almost a year since the magnificent, yet sad funeral services for Secretary Brown. I can't help wondering—why I still find snippets of information (sources unknown) in my daily newspaper about once per month stating shit like Washington–Doctor: *"Autopsy was in order a military medical examiner said Thursday that an autopsy should have been performed on Commerce Secretary Brown to investigate a suspicious skull wound after he died in a plane crash in Croatia"*. Oh those suspicious wounds, I believe next month or next year, it'll be a gunshot wound, seen by a (deceased) eyewitness! Why must we black folks be tortured so, all we ever ask for is the truth coming out of Washington–anytime soon? I doubt it! Even though 1.8 million blacks came together on October 16, 1995 in peace and unity on the White House lawn, nearly 4,500,000 (more or less-my estimate) who could have and should have been there, simply took their black asses back to work. Secretary Brown will forever be missed. God rest his soul—my own soul is truly pissed off!

Enough said for now–in closing I'd like to add, "*to all those so-called educated and conservative blacks in this country, (they know who they are), who truly believe that our government (or the ruling power elite) would never sanction the intentional death and destruction of 35-40 white and black business men, just to eliminate one important and powerful blackman—there is absolutely no excuse for your unbridled ignorance! Study white European history over the last 500 years, and while you're at it study some black history in America, for just the last 300 years!*" Then will you believe?—I doubt it! What did the old slave-master say to Old-Fiddler in the movie Roots when he caught him thinking seriously about freedom and independence? "*Stop that! Take your black-ass back to work*"... and Fiddler did! Many of us followed him that day and many of us today will ask no questions of old master Uncle Sam, but will simply take our black asses back to work—Damn!

AN URGENT WARNING TO WHITE AMERICA

Old white America—Please heed these solemn words of warning: Yes, I've finished creating and venting—much which will be perceived as old news, some of which might be new to you, all of which screams out to you to please take your foot off the necks of black Americans!

Yes, it still seems too many of us (black folks) that we cannot live apart from you, yet it also seems true that we still can't live with you. Still, my message (within this book's pages) has been a plea for peace and toleration, because we don't need your love—but we do need your cooperation. It (this book) has been a plea for understanding and compassion against the pains of continued racial injustices and the evil of discrimination against people of color. Be aware that much of our mutual problems is based on a lack of trusting one another, and the continued teaching of your children (but not ours) the principles of hate, prejudices, and intolerance. This must stop at some point and that point is now!

What have you have been taught about us (black folks)? and by whom? Your parents, your loved ones, your racist ancestors? And what do you think you've learned about us from the six o'clock news, your biased newspapers and magazines that continue to slight and focus only on the negative aspects of a people—my people! Just what do we (black folks) continue to learn about you (white folks) in this great country of ours? Why is it that the daily experiences for most of my people here in America is one of pain, racial suffering, degradation, humiliation, discrimination, physical assault, false arrest, racial manipulation, insensitive racial remarks and insults, and abundant negative images and symbols of our presumed inherent inferiority?

Why indeed are our churches and bridges toward one another still burning? Why are burning Christian crosses still lighting the nights in some suburban areas, when a black family moves in, and swastika-symbols still being painted on black peoples properties all across America? It seems the destiny of two peoples (our races) is being manipulated by some towards a race-war in this country, and if an internal war in this country is our mutual destiny—then so be it! Just be aware of the dire consequences! Be aware of our love (black people, brown people, red people) for our freedom today! It is as strong as ever, and no one racial-side shall win in this kind of battle! There will be no victors in such a war because when the scorched earth runs red with blood, it will be the mutual blood of all our children and not just the blood of the black ones ,or the little red ones as was the case only a hundred years ago! Blacks today will not be forced to live on reservations!

White America please be reminded—it truly seems that many of us (black folks) are very tired of saying—of warning our enemies, tired even of preaching the real gospel of being black in America, a very painful gospel. For many of us it is still a hell-on-earth, steeped in racial hatred and injustices not of our own making! I see something coming, a dark cloud of frustration, a widespread sense of total and massive exasperation from a people who are loosing their collective patience with the monsters of hate and death the white man's inhumanity toward his darker-skinned brothers! Again, white America must stop pushing black people around so hard, and cease trying to turn an intelligent and hardworking, patriotic people in to a permanent second-class, under-class, subservient class of people like they (we) were just 75 years ago!

Please allow me to break you white folks off a little something-something! Do you have any idea how many millions (yes, millions) of blacks—right here in this country (the U.S.A.) who are "*today*" silently screaming "d*on't push me, I'm close to the edge, I'm trying so hard not to lose my head.*" Where they constantly wonder how they can keep from going under! White America, yes, I am as amazed as you must be. At how few blacks in this climate of hopelessness have been found guilty of committing a post-office style assault on their fellow white American oppressors and racist enemies. It seems to me that even a domesticated dog will bite back (fight back), when it sees it's young offspring (and itself) continuously being threatened with potential death and destruction. Question. Why shouldn't black people feel even more outraged! Daily we (black folks) hear so much negative reporting by the white media, (read Dr. Ofrie Hutchinson's book The Assassination of the Black Male Image) that for many of us after years of this kind of mental-crippling, bullshit programming, we no longer wish to be identified with out own race! It's true!

Daily, we here the shocking statistics. We question why our young black men between the ages of 15 and 28 have a lower life expectancy (survival rate) than any other racial group in America! (A few brave voices have been raised lately to sound an alarm, but they too, are being ignored). Will someone please explain to black folks once and for all, what is the real definitive answer to the question of how and why are drugs continuing to run rampant in the black communities all across America? It's a known fact that black people don't grow, produce, process, or ship large quantities of drugs into this country of ours! It seems that black people in general all over this country, continue to receive less than adequate healthcare and emergency room treatment (when it is often badly needed) than their white counterparts, at the same hospitals! Why? why? why?

Why are millions of hardworking, law abiding blacks still steered and redlined into certain suburban areas (usually recently vacated by fleeing whites) when buying homes, searching for better schools and areas of less crime? Why does white America (if you please, elements thereof) never tire of reminding black people in hundreds of insulting and insensitive ways of their very blackness? As if any other group (race) in America is as conscious of their (obvious) genetic birth-marker of color, then black folks? Black people are probably the only group of Americans who awake each and every morning, without having to look into some mirror to know that they are indeed different. They awake each day with a consciousness of color, their blackness! Having been taught by others, and having accepted the fact (negatively) that being black in America comes with a heavy price, the price of a possible early death, or jail sentence, if we forget our place in society, a very real price, even today. Yet a price many of our people have gladly paid for freedom and equality before many of us were even born. For the right to be free of cruel and harsh punishment, the freedom of speech, the pursuit of life, liberty, and equal treatment under the laws of this land. The right to vote and run for any public office, and most of all, to possess apart of the great American dream! In it's many advertised facets and forms that white people for years have enjoyed in abundance all over America! So I ask again, please white America, take your foot off the necks of black Americans! Move it or lose it!

Yes, there are many of us over thirty-five, who remember our fallen Black heroes of yesterday like Reginald Lewis, Ron Brown, Malcolm and Martin (and worry over those that shall come) and those of recent days. Truly it was not too long ago when we grieved for our brothers and sisters, during the equal rights and civil-rights era—who were murdered in this country often times by our own Government's Security Forces. Solely, because they were black and fearless. Those who saw the very real need to stand up and fight back against a brutally racist and oppressive white culture, one that absolutely feared and despised their darker-skinned brothers and sisters. Calling them dangerous decedents of ex-slaves and naked savages of a strange and distant land to justify killing and incarcerating their young! Four-hundred years of this shit is enough!

We have not forgotten the Philadelphia Movement? And their intentional destruction by being bombed out of existence because they wore the last name of "*Africa*!" Many of us recall their unwarranted deaths at the order of a black Mayor Goode—who was lied to and used by white police officials (who told him it was just tear gas). What of the fiery death of our brother Cinque and the Symbolnese Liberation Army—out in California who never received a real chance to surrender (but Patty Hurst somehow survived). We have our memories of the Black community's only true "armed security force." The late and great Black Panther Party. We can say the names of the party's great leaders like Huey, Eldridge, Hampton, and Seale and others. It seems that after more recent atrocities and unwarranted murders by white policemen (and white racist) in our communities of late, I and many others, have come to the end of our hope-rope! White American racists and hate-mongers must be warned, one last time! The clock is ticking, your time is running out and so is the patience of millions of Black men and women in this country. These words are now welling up inside sore throats and pushing uncontrollably through the bruised and tightened lips of many frustrated young and old Blacks alike. To say—"*stop fucking over Black Americans—or face the dire consequences!*"

If white America (or elements thereof) don't begin to truly police itself, and stop the indiscriminate killing of innocent/passive/non-violent blacks. The day may soon come where no warning will be given, and Hell will begin to exist on the surface of the earth and not below it! Again, you've been warned white America! Now go and rent the movie (video) "*Falling Down*" and substitute Morgan Freeman's face for that of Michael Douglas' face, then multiply that angry Black face by 25-30 million angry black faces (50% of us). Do you , White America get the picture? I truly hope so! I really, truly hope so! Any child can pull a trigger and mistakenly kill his brother, but a frustrated race knows how to aim, at it's overconfident enemies! Remember Vietnam's victory over America's war machine? Many black vets and I remember! Could this happen in America? I hope not, I pray it does not! So white America, you've been warned! Is anybody white listening? "*We be sick too, mas-ser can be replaced with, we all gon fall down mas-ser, we all (blacks and whites) be falling down!*" Damn it! "*If just one more black leader dies under mysterious circumstances, or some innocent black person dies simply because of the color of their skin, then it shouldn't come as no surprise if two or three innocent whites mysteriously meet up with the same fate!*" Is anybody white listening? Will we be hearing America's white children crying, screaming, saying, "*we all gon fall down—we be sick to Uncle Sam.*" Damn, Damn, must we all be damned? Maybe so, before white America will listen and repent! I scream- freedom and equality for all or freedom for none, fuck it! I'm tired of just my people falling down! I'm tired white America—I'm so tired, and I'm not alone!

I JUST MIGHT CATCH A CASE

Hell yeah—I'm angry, I beg your pardon? I'm mad as hell!

If just one more damn high rate, red-lining, premium-gorging, inner-city auto insurance company tries to stick me up just because I choose to live and drive in a black city, I just might catch a case!

If just one more white landlord or white realty company denies me access to a decent apartment or home again, just because I'm a black person. I do think I might just catch me a case!

If just one more Jehovah's Witness rings my damn doorbell again—early on Saturday morning, while I'm trying to recover from a hectic week of fighting with white-folks and niggers. I truly believe I just might catch a case!

If just one more Arab or Chaldean market owner tries his best to sell me some more spoiled or rotten meat, while refusing to place my change back into my hands—as if I'm dirty. Then I know I just might catch a case!

If just one more white security guard at the mall follows me around and/or hassles me again, because I like to wear jogging-suits and fresh gym shoes while shopping. I believe I just might catch me a case—I also shop where I live!

If just one more juvenile delinquent (homie) attempts to jack my jeep out of my driveway early in the morning when it's parked right next to my damn house and I'm getting in it. I just might catch me a case!

If just one more police academy rookie pulls me over again because he thinks I shouldn't be driving an expensive truck with darkly tinted windows—where he can't see inside. I really think I just might catch a case!

If just one more of my white co-workers asks me again, if I really believe O.J. Simpson is innocent or guilty of murder, without mentioning Mr. Mark Furhman. I know I'm going to catch me a case!

If just one more "brother-man" asks me at the gas station—if he can clean my windows or pump my gas for some spare change (because he says he'll work for food) all-the-while looking as if he's eating for two people, I truly believe I just might catch a case.

Truly it's easy to catch a criminal case—if you be black, living and driving in the big city, while wearing a jogging suit and gym shoes, in a Jeep with dark windows, shopping for some meat now-a-days! Just what the hell is the world coming to? Or is this just another Urban-American nightmare? Snap! There goes my mind! Damn... I've caught me a case! "Yoh moma—get Johnny Cocahren on the phone, please!"

*Dedicated to a black man (an unsung black hero) named Mr. French an ex-union rep at Ford Motor Company who didn't want to hear the word "nigger" again flowing from the lips of a white union associate, and who just caught a murder case at the ripe old age of 52 at a surburban auto plant west of Detroit. The fault lies entirely in the hands of Mr. French's black-ass designer suit wearing-wanna be white attorney! Who took Mr. French's money for his defense, but stated "he didn't need to play the race card, because race was only a side issue in the case". (just like Christopher Dardin at OJ's circus). Acting like he never heard of jury-nullification, or saving a black client from a biased legal system at any cost wasn't his damn job! it happens everyday in courtrooms all over America. Race matters damn it! And we know this! We need to support those brothers going to court - before our fucking turn comes around! "No more state funded GED classes for jail inmates, old Governors say". Look for another Attica-style massacre coming soon to your local prison one day... remember I told you. Damn predictions - bet!

THINK

Dear brothers and sisters (to all my beautiful and civilized black jewels) with your permission, might I share with you this simple yet profound admonition... please continue to think! Think now! Do it today and each and every day until you die! Do it now! Thinking may become illegal soon! Especially if you're black and truly intelligent in America. Because intelligent thinking blacks (especially those with PhDs wearing kente-cloth so proudly) still seem to be a threat to most of White America. But, never allow this to frighten you into not continuing to think! Bet! Question-Just what could we 50-60 million black adult minds (minus 5-10 million who are absent without permission) all thinking together, accomplish in this country for our people by the year 2005? Remember, no thinking ventured, nothing is gained. What couldn't we accomplish if we all thought the same... whooah!

JUST THINK?

PETTY, PETTY, MOTHER-FUCKERS

When it comes down to people in general, and specifically my own people, there's nothing more irritating and distressing to me than a simple-minded, petty motherfucker! Here's an unfortunate example—yeah it's true, some of my people (the niggers amongst us) that are presently incarcerated in jails around the country—actually come to blows (fighting) over a kool-aide type drink! Only four-ounces, artificially flavored, and served at room temperature! So let's call them what they have chosen to be, Petty motherfuckers! Wait-wait! Some of my people (niggers) even out of jail actually come to blows over he said-she said, she say-he say shit! No known facts, no explanations given, no time spent checking out the rumors or accusations! So, let us call them too what they have chosen to be, simple-minded, petty motherfuckers! Yes those poor souls (or soul-less) people/persons who would risk life and limb just to appear tuff, fit this title. Who in turn, both males and females, will probably end up in the white man's jails somewhere in America, (black people don't build jails, not enough black contractors or skilled tradesmen- we're told—we just help to pay for them) fighting over a kool-aid drink, damn! You mean you shot a brother because he <u>scratched</u> your new car? My mistake—he disrespected your child by calling him (or her) a half-breed. No? oh, so she cut in front of you at the check-cashing depot and you stabbed her?—don't lie to me P.M.F., don't lie! So he took a long drag on your last cigarette, or, the last swig on your 40 oz. so you killed him! Talk about a petty, motherfucker! Its true, petty motherfuckers can come in <u>any</u> sex or size, in any race or disguise! We must strive to avoid petty-minded people—for their disease is often very contagious and dangerous. You've been warned–Bet!

COMMUNITY LAW ENFORCEMENT

How nice (safe) it would be in this country—if law enforcement agencies would truly accept and respect black Americans human and civil rights, as much (even as much) as they respect and protect White Americans human and civil rights! Granted—we black folk have come along way since slavery-times, when it was OK to catch, convict, and punish black-folks just for being black and in the wrong place at the wrong time (or for not having white folks permission to be anywhere). Still we must agree, we have a long way to go—and any fight is never over until the fight is won or lost. Many of us still wonder (because many of us intentionally avoid this question) which out-come would we rather have! ... Who amongst black-folks will be the next victim—of the dangerous day or deadly night at the hands of racist policemen or sheriff's deputies still patrolling urban city streets? How many cops does it take to subdue a drunken Rodney King, or to kill an unarmed Malice Green? ... Since when did a toilet-plunger up a brother's rectum, become N.Y.P.D.'s new prisoner control-tactic?! Will my father—or your mother, my sister—or your brother be next? Yes I'm praying for these three assaulted brothers, just like many others. Translate Justice to Just-Us! Criminal laws and profiling may be color blind, but their application on the streets of urban America is not!

My main man Mr. George Clinton of P-Funk fame (a true visionary), warns us at his recent sold-out concerts—Black Funk-A-Teers (10% of us) better beware of martial-law, I think I know why–cause–if a real race-war ever hits America, we'd better hit our local jails and prisons first, to liberate the many urban guerrillas—(no pun intended)—being housed inside America jails and prisons. America has locked down many political prisoners of color these days ... This is where we will find most of our true warriors, because we know most of them will fight—and some would be willing even to kill again. Unlike many of us on the out-side, who may be too passive and civilized—too educated by white power to do otherwise! Answer-Up! Whose policing our communities… are we? Are you? Oh yes, it won't be long—before jails and prisons in America, all become privatized. (They are already on the NYS Exchange). I predict—when they do, a 100% rise in the lock-up rate of young black lives (with 11 year olds being tried as adults already)—our future progeny becoming the new source of slave labor! Again, how nice (safe) it would truly be in this country—if law enforcement agencies would just chill, … . and stop the black over kill! … … Bet! Fact: "our brother Abdul Muima Jamal did not receive a fair trial in Philadelphia—period! So set him free damn it! See it for yourself, go rent the video "Muima–An American Injustice" –Bet!

BLACKS ON T.V. AND RADIO TALK SHOWS

My people, my people—suckers! Fools! Damn Dummies! Traitors! Where in the hell have you been? Where have you and your people lived for the last 300 years or so? Why don't you know you're being played (used and abused) by the white "*Boob tube-Media*"? If anybody ask you or any of your loved ones anyone of these (dumb-ass) personal and very private questions, please tell them to get the hell out of your face! If they really want an answer to these derogatory and highly insulting questions, then they should go and ask their mothers! Stay with me now, it gets better!

My people, my people—suckers! Fools! Damn Dummies! Traitors! Peep this shit! See it for what it really is! Wake uuuppp! Does your mother compete with you (her teenage daughter) for your teenage boyfriend? Are you and your sister/cousin sleeping with the same man? Are you and your present lover brother and sister? Are you a sex-slave to your spouse? Do you (at 14) and your mother (at 30) hang out in the park with the same boys (or men) for money? Have you or someone you know fallen in love with the man (or woman) who raped you when you were younger? Does your mom, best girlfriend, or sister wear tight fitting sexy clothes while being 40-60 pounds overweight? Does your gay brother or bisexual sister (mother or father) flaunt their sexuality out in public? Geez, almighty!

My people, my people—suckers! Fools! Damn Dummies! Traitors! You must answer these types of questions in only one way! You must say it's truly none of yours or anyone else's damned business ... period! Brain check, please! There are still those in the media (print, radio, and T.V.) who want to use and abuse you (especially black folks to further type cast, stereotype, cast dispersions, and subtly embarrass you and your whole race. They know all-too-well that the general T.V. viewing audience will easily believe what applies to you will also apply to all of your people—your race! If you have no shame, no self-respect, no decency, no morals, no parenting skills, little or no education, or no awareness of your people's great history or no sense of your own spirituality, no self control, nothing truly important to say, then you don't need to get your black asses up on national T.V, and show your true ignorance, or perverted behavior for all of America to see, hear and laugh at! I am truly ashamed of those of my brothers and sisters who already have! Shame on all of them!

My people, my people- suckers! Fools! Damn Dummies! Traitors! How utterly unreal, how utterly stupid and how disgusting for anyone to stand in front of a T.V. camera or mike and talk about why they sell dope, are gang-bangers, robbed or raped another human being (especially black people) or why you killed a goat in a satanic ritual, committed incest, bigamy, body-piercing, a sexual perversion, married a white racist hate monger, who calls you his nigger spouse! And then you have the gall to expound upon the virtues of the constitution and the freedom of speech, all the while setting the worse example of a bad, negative, sadistic, perverted, and erroneous image of an example of your race! Blacks must come to realize (especially all of you manipulated Hollywood wannabes) that you hurt more than yourselves. You also hurt your families, personal friends, your race, your great heritage, your people's hard won and courageous history. Lacking any self respect and dignity will only increase your individual sufferings after the dastardly deed has been done (your appearing on Jenny Jones, Jerry Springer, and the like). Yes, you may even lose your life after appearing on one of these trash talk shows? So stop it! Stop this madness—just don't go! Never participate in your own peoples' oppression (especially if you are black and claim to be proud of your beautiful, genetic birthright). Never give in and sell out! Don't ever let your beautiful black image that was fought for and earned by many great black people to uplift you and I, and our overall image of black people. Even be assaulted or degraded by anyone! From the very evil, false and negative images, created and used by white America's media machine to keep black people down and feeling inferior to all other races and nationalities here in America. Dig this, the perception of a people is more valuable than gold. We need to recognize this fact!

My people, my people –Suckers! Fools! Damn Dummies! Traitors! If you, or someone you know are black, and about to go on national T.V. or a radio talk show (who can barely speak good English or who thinks the word "*PI*" stands for sweet potatoes) and they can't tell you when Martin Luther King Jr. was born or when Malcolm X was killed or that Niki Giovanni is a great poet, or that Angela Davis was a great black civil rights warrior, or that Rosa Parks will always refuse to give up her bus sit to a white man, do whatever it takes to stop them! Foolish and stupid blacks sought after by radio and television are as great a threat to the health and welfare, the positive self-images of all intelligent and proud black people everywhere as any boot licking, ass-kissing, tap-dancing, skinning and grinning, wannabe white Uncle Thomas or Aunt Jemima domesticated servant of the black race could ever be! If I could, I surely would push a button on all black T.V./radio puppets all across the land and zap their black asses right out of this universe! Since this can't be done yet, I'll just continue to exercise my intelligence and turnoff any media tool that's used to demean and destroy the very souls of my people! All black people should feel this way. Please don't watch or listen to this mentally crippling kind of shit on T.V. or the radio! Please stop participating in this great sham of so called entertainment! No matter how much money they (you know who "*they*" are) offer you. Our basic self-respect and self-love should never be up for sale for any price! We'd better recognize!

My people, my people—suckers! Fools! Damn Dummies! Traitors! Collectively, "*we*" cannot afford the life threatening results that will surely come and disastrously affect the very struggles of our black children for a decent life here in a predominate white racist America! If we continue to debase our race on T.V. talk shows or radio or even on the streets!

Remember if you will what the late great Marcus Garvey said to black Americans not long ago, inside his National Negro Digest… *"if Negro Americans ever want to be treated equal to white American in this land of former slaves and slave-masters, then all Negro Americans need to retrain their minds and restrain themselves from saying or doing anything that can be used to further debase and destroy black*

Americans. 'This would be a start!'" Enough said, go ahead watch what you must on your TV then watch what Geraldo and Montel (yes, Montel is a tool) has to say about you and our people after you leave their studios! Then remember, what I and brother Marcus Garvey tried to tell you, and don't let me be standing by and see your faces when you come to the rude awakening that the only good nigger for T.V. and radio, and the movies (that exploits) is the one that entertains white America with a dance, a joke or a negative stereotype of his or her own people! Unless you can run a football like Barry Sanders, or slam a basketball like Grant Hill, then and only then might I join you in watching a little telly! Watching talent at work is entertaining, watching trash T.V. is not! Shit, we got a lot of work to do together, so watch on my people, watch on! Go ahead and play that funky music white boy. Black TV talk show people (puppets), whatever shall we do with you? I damn sho know what I would like to do with shameless, ignorant blacks on TV talk shows, but it's against the whiteman's law for now! Consider the greater question, "*what will come of black pseudo-actors and black entertainers of white racist America, when they are no longer entertained or amused by them*," oh, I shudder to think! Sometimes, now-a-days, the hangman's rope and slave whip come disguised as a T.V. camera and microphone! Bet and true that, wake up black America! Damn it—just wake up and walk tall with pride again!

OH THAT BLACK SICKNESS

Despite what we're continuously told about our salt intake, lack of physical exercise, and other contemporary lifestyle taboos—fully 90% of high-blood pressure cases have no known cause. (Damn, is this true?) Still, Blacks, Cubans and Puerto Ricans (I also suspect Mexican-Americans) are three times more likely to suffer from high-blood pressure, heart disease, and depression, than Anglo-Americans. Don't take my word for it, call your local American Heart Association. How much is one phone call?

I know what makes me sick as a black man today, it's those damn TV-commercials for businesses and fast food franchises that use prize winning promotions (like scratch and win games), where every other race of people wins big cash, or a big home, or an exotic trip, and the brother or sister (black) wins only a damn hamburger or supersize fries! Worse yet, my blood-pressure skyrockets, when a black teenage cashier or waitress acts like I caused her cramps, or kicked his dog, and I have to restrain myself from wanting to choke the shit out of one of them—after demanding my money back! Thank God I have patience and love for black folks, even the young, misguided ones!

Truly, it's not all their fault that so many of them behave this way. Somewhere, elder-blacks (parents included) allowed them to be raised to be disrespectful and mean-spirited toward their own families and other blacks. Back in the day, a green tree switch would have changed all this. "*Oh that black sickness. I believe it's due to two-legged white germs and even more to white lies!*" Bet. Quick! Somebody bring me my Casta-oil and a lemon. Hold back that "*Jew-Jew*" Powder! Damn sickness! Just makes me sick!

STATISTICS AND POLLS

Isn't it amazing and even astounding—that no matter how much wealth, or power, or hard won fame and fortune a black person gains in "Our America." This person is still whispered to be a black-fluke, or just another lucky Nigger? It is said that nearly 75—80% of white Americans are secretly feeling this way. Statistics and polls don't lie, or do they, and if they do lie on occasion, and we know that they often do, shouldn't this be against the law? Damn—this could go on forever! My brothers and sisters—please don't believe everything you read (put out for the general unenlightened masses), or hear especially statistics and polls. Statistics and polls—are like pimps and hoes, one takes your money, while the other gets sold! Neither one is trustworthy worth a damn and you know this… bet!

BLACK ALIENS

What if those alien bodies recovered by the U.S. Air Force back in 1947 out in the desert of Roswell, New Mexico, wearing blackish-blue jump suits were actually the bodies of some young black space explorers from an all black planet! Remember—there were no black faces, but plenty of black spaces in the block-buster Star Wars Trilogy—until someone with a conscious, pointed this out to Mr. George Lucas, and he decided to remedy this large oversight by casting the best looking negro he could find. Presto—magic—Billy D. Williams out of forced retirement! Hell yeah – when they (white people) need us, they will come bearing all sorts of gifts and promises! Better watch your back Mr. Will Smith—true Independence Day in America has not arrived for black people yet! Question: would a true black alien speak alienese or ebonics? Well, I bet our government knows which! Shit—I know some brothers and sisters today, who act like black aliens! They swear up and down they've never eaten collard-greens, don't like fried-chicken, have never been exposed to overt racism or discrimination by whites! What if those alien bodies discovered by the U.S. Air Force back in 1947, were the grandparents of some of today's black-ass-aliens (sell outs)! It would surely explain a lot, wouldn't it ... Bet! Somebody get me some grits, but hold the bacon. I can't hunt black aliens on a empty stomach! Fact: Black Americans are still treated like black aliens by the majority of white-ass Americans. What gall! What nerve! What unadulterated bull-shit black aliens embrace, just to fit in and feel like they belong somewhere..damn! "*The black Gods from Osirus*" would not be amused... read the book!

WHOOPI'S APPARENT IDENTITY CRISIS

Ms. Goldberg—you know you should be ashamed girl! Why is it that, whenever some members of our race gain fame, wealth, or great rewards—beyond what they ever dreamed possible here in America, they appear suddenly overcome by some kind of success sickness and identity crisis?—Damn! We know what the hell I'm talking about here. Folks like Ms. Whoopi, Ms. J. Jackson, Mr. C. Thomas, Mr. Monty Williams, and W. Connelly to name a few.

Is it simply the money? Is there something about presumed wealth, or new found status (like 1 or 2 million dollars or 1 or 2 million copies sold) that causes a black man or black woman to believe they can then flirt with inter-racial disaster (like the Juice)? These brothers and sisters seem hell bent on having themselves a member of the opposite sex, of another race as their spouses or latest love interest, knowing full-well ahead of time this is still one of America's greatest taboos! Why oh why won't somebody tell me—why these confused blacks with all their new wealth or recognition, won't marry or fall in love with one of their own race? I honestly think I know why. Please somebody go dig up old evil bones "*Mr. Willie Lynch*", I know he'll have some answers from over 250 years ago – bet. *"Gentlemen, I have the keys for controlling your negro slaves for well over 300 years to come. Take the visible differences between your slaves and make them bigger, like their hair, skin-shade, size, sex, and ages. Teach them first and foremost to fear you, then to hate and despise themselves. Use envy, jealousy and distrust for control purposes. Let me assure you, that conditioned distrust of their own race is stronger then adulation, and fear of white's retribution works better than respect and admiration. Keeping in mind that after your black slaves have become so properly indoctrinated with these principles, they shall carry on and become self-loathing, self-refueling and self-generating for hundreds of years, maybe even thousands. They must love, respect, and trust only us (their white masters).* Damn! I'm beginning to see the light said the blind man.

Now, back to black America's latest black-ass sell-out. Oh hell yeah—I heard her interview on the radio a few months ago with my own ears, talking about how she "*no-longer wanted to be identified (or referred to) as a black-American or Afro-American*"… she went on to say, "*I don't know anything about Africa or my ancestors, all I know is that my grandmother was born in the south of these United States*". Damn, well I just can't help myself. Ms. Whoopi—just what the hell were you thinking? Surely you know by now why white folks love you, support you, and promote you! Because you, my dark chocolate sister, represent to them the definitive black American stereotype of that "*lady on those cornmeal bags*", who just recently was allowed to take that red rag off of her head she had worn since the late fifties and sixties.

You'll probably come to understand one day my little star, my utter disgust, and deep disappointment with you and other modern day black sell-outs. After your very own "*white Bronco chase*" down L.A.'s freeways, when you're forced to return to the hood! Speaking of your roots in the hood—back in the early days when you were hungry, you were unafraid to tell the hard-core truth about white folks (albeit in a humorous way). Now that you've made a little money and moved to the suburbs, you don't want to be known as a "black American"—just as an American. Damn! Well girlfriend, personally I liked you better when you were on welfare. At least back then you knew you were black! Many black and proud Americans and their children were listening to you that day on the radio. All I can say now is "*shame on you nigger—shame on you*!" True black Americans have got to start holding negro sell-outs, Uncle Toms/Aunt Jemima blacks accountable as co-conspirators and traitors to the very survival of black people everywhere. They know the damage and hurt they inflict on their own race—they know and yet, they're no longer afraid to sell us all out. Maybe they need to be – bet!

LOST HOPE

"*A mind is a terrible thing to waste*". I keep hearing this, but so is a heart—right? Isn't it also true that in order to be loved—one must be willing to risk being loving? We (black folks) must embrace our own rich heritage, and those old black values that have brought us through some of the toughest times in America. We (black folks) must once again fix (reprogram) our minds and strengthen our hearts (by practicing group love again) for our own people, especially the little ones. The future will judge us so harshly—if only a few of us (and not the whole race) arrive to meet her! I'd like to believe that we (black people) shall survive the coming of the "*New World Order*", but only if we unite as one people, one tribe, with one heart, and one mind! So let us all pray to whatever God we love.

Let us all pray that it is not too late for God's meekest children. Let us pray we have not lost our fighting spirit, or courage to stand strong together. Will you all pray with me, that for whatever reason we all don't lose our hope. For if we (black folks) lose our hope, then indeed we all will surely be lost in the belly of the whale (the USA) forever! "*A mind is a terrible thing to waste*" I keep hearing this—but so is a people right? More love for our race, our own people, is the simple key. Lost hope is not an option! From the book Dirty Little Secrets by Dr. Claude Anderson—(p.183) "*The CDC reported in the 1980's that being black in America means higher mortality rates than any other race, lower levels of education, occupational status, incomes, wealth, health, housing, fewer two-parent households, higher unemployment and greater contact with the criminal justice system among blacks, to a large degree, stems directly from the structural economic and social inequalities produced by centuries of slavery, Jim Crowism and benign neglect.*"

Black men are still the primary target of racism today and therefore, still at risk of "lost hope and hazardous health!". Let us re-define "*endangered species*" let us defend our hope!

OH THAT TIGER WOODS AND THE NEXT CENSUS

Question, tell me my brothers and sisters, who else besides myself has seen our brother, "*Mr. Golf*" (young Tiger Woods) on the evening news lately being interviewed and always being asked this question, "Mr. Woods, how do you describe yourself, I mean your nationality, you know, race-wise?" (I always wonder why white folks always bring up race or race-issues whenever they interview one of our black heroes or celebrities on national T.V. It seems to me they're just waiting for a slip-up of some kind dealing with the issue of race or it's negative impact as it relates to the concerns of the white-elite and blacks in this country). So tell us, Mr. Woods, which race do you feel closest to? Of course, young Mr. Woods aims to please his fans and constituency, there's a great deal at stake (usually a great deal of endorsement monies) so one must be polite and cautious, so as not to offend the ruling class. Young Mr. Woods usually responds to these types of questions from the media by saying something like, "*I guess I'm what you could call a Casblasian.*" You see, I have some white, some black and some Asian mixtures (blood-lines) tied together within me. Well, well, well, here we go again, with the needed education of one of our own, about the real racist nature of white people in particular and old white racist America in general. No, I'm not going to ask an obvious question like, why is it whenever some black person (in appearance) gets up on national T.V. or radio and ascribes to being identified with anything, any other race, nationality, or culturally other than their dark-skinned brothers and sisters back in the black-ass hood. They make themselves look foolish and unintelligent. What I would ask these types of multi-ethnic folks, is simply this, why is it so damn hard or wrong for you to just say, "*Hey, I'm a black person, a black American, and I'm truly proud of that*?"

In contrast we all know how easy it is for white people to quickly claim their white heritage, don't we? Most black folks in this day and age know that they have all kinds of mixed bloodlines running through their veins, cause we come in a multitude of hues, hair and eye-color variations, yet we also know (those of us with a beautiful, black consciousness) that white folks have never made allowances or true acceptance for anyone that they have considered of mixed-blood. It was even one of their laws not too long ago that if a person had one drop of black blood in their bodies —even if it didn't show—they were still considered to be black and banished to the black side of town! Even today many white folk still feel the same way. Here's proof – even though Mr. Woods tells white American that he's a Casblasian (whatever the hell that is), white America as represented by Scuzzy Zoeller, (one example among many) generally responds by assuming a Casblasian eats fried chicken, and collard greens like any other black person in America. How untrue and racist. Young Mr. Tiger probably prefers Thai food.

Now, it's also a fact that blacks have always had a different feeling for our brothers and sisters of mixed-race heritage. For much of our captive existence here in this country, blacks have exhibited a more tolerant and loving acceptance of our light-skinned kin. Why is this? Traditionally, black folks were not too quick to label, to ostracize one of our own. We have hardly ever turned against the isolated, lonely mulatto (fair-skin-white-featured) brother or sister, even during slavery times. Who more often than not was still treated like family, by the slave ancestors and freedmen because they had that 1 oz. of black blood. Even today, most educated and intelligent blacks still accept our mixed-race brothers and sisters easily who lay claim to being part American-Indian or anything else, because it's truly their personal right to do so. I suspect that for most of us we're just not as prejudiced as our white counterparts. Being less inclined, I suppose to take notice of that indomitable black gene (even watered down) that refuses to be faded, except in Michael Jackson's case. I know how sad its going to be for most of our younger cross-over brothers and sisters (and the young Tiger) when they finally become exposed to the truth of what I'm speaking of here. You see it everyday, where white-ass Americans take every opportunity to remind black-wannabe-white and black-born chameleons of their genetic inherited inferiority, especially if they're sporting a deep natural tan like Mr. Woods. Now again, I don't fault young Tiger Woods for his self-identifying racial preference. I fault his father, an obvious intelligent and military trained blackman, who I'm sure knows damn well that white America and most of the white world still racially categorizes one's progeny (children) according to the race (or ethnicity) of the father, ever since the first Bible was written.

For many black Americans, there is still some serious racial lessons for them to learn from white folks. There are still some bitter pills that must be swallowed. Lesson number one, "*not your fame, nor your talent, nor your money, or your title, will cause us (white folks) to see you in any other way than the one that served us so well over the last 400 years! If you look black to us, you'll be black to us and therefore inferior!*" Well now this brings me to another important facet of contemporary American life. Just what are we to make of the plans to change the next great census count, coming to America at the turn of the century?! The headlines continue to shout "*It's about time*" (is it?)—so the country's census bureau is making provisions to contain new racial categories for people of mixed races. Check this shit out will you? Our government is planning to add new multiracial categories in the next U.S. census, where Americans of mixed ancestry will be able to list themselves in as many racial categories as applies to them. Damn, I wonder what old racist Uncle Sam is really up to now? Traditionally, we were limited to just one of the current categories of black, white, American-Indian, Alaska Native, or Asian or Pacific Islander. Now it's claimed by the government census planners, that in recent years, due to the growth in the number of mixed-race people and their racially mixed up children, these new categories are needed. The number of children in mixed-race families have jumped from fewer than 500,000 to 2.5 million from 1970 to 1995. I personally believe that all <u>mixed-race people and black folks in general</u> had better beware of this new governmental strategy to create a new "*minority-class*" in America, and at the same time lower the number of total black folks in this country (killing two birds with one stone). Most intelligent and aware black Americans know that the census count affects statistics that are used to redistrict seats in Congress and the legislature and used in the study of economic and social trends here in America. It seems that these new changes about to take place in the next census, may have some serious ulterior motives behind them! To all my mixed-race brothers and sisters who may be confused about which category to check off, I want you to know that Big Brother Earl truly respects your right to take pride in recognition of your mixed-race heritage. But don't be surprised if and when the time comes for you to chose a racial category on the next census, you mark the box Casblasian and still, your white neighbor hollers across the street at you.

"Hey boy, yeah you with the watermelon grin and the golf-clubs, wanna go shoot 9 or 18 holes this Saturday?" Tell him yes, if his trailer-trash possum-eating, hillbilly mother can be your caddy. Bet! Play it safe and smart mark the box that says black American only—if not, you may regret it later. Ya'll don't want to be a new minority in America—cause minorities suffer to much!

RELATIONSHIPS AND COMMUNICATION

My people, know this, whenever a black woman says to her black man, *"I ain't trying to hear that shit (actually hear him)"*, then that relationship is over!

Whenever a black man says to his black woman, *"You are one stupid bitch, shut the fuck-up"*, then that relationship is over! Way over!

Whenever a black woman tells her black man, *"You think you know every damn thing, so don't ask me shit!"* Then that relationship is over and we know it!

Whenever black men and black women can no longer communicate with one another (taking turns), one talking while the other one truly listens, then that relationship is over! Most problems in relationships is indeed caused by a lack of communication between concerned parties. If black people keep in mind that conversation and communication is a two-way flow of information and ideas, supported by mutual respect, then most problems in relationships would disappear.

What of race relations in America? Well, whenever a black man stands with a white man (i.e., the Republican—so called moral majority party), over another black man, or whenever a black woman stand with a white woman (i.e., the National Organization of Women—Right to Life Party), over another black woman, then those relationships are way passed being over! Here we become unconscious witnesses and participants to the further decline of the black race (over time) into a race of invisible people, then that relationship (race) is over! American is a long way from being color blind. I know invisible people can't be seen, but they can see!

My people know this, whenever we fail to communicate with one of our own people, we should never attempt to build a relationship with an outsider of another race of people, because mutual respect is still absent coming from white people in general, and white racist Americans in particular. So make that second or third attempt. We must remain united as a people!

If you're a black man or woman in this country, I'm sure you'll come to agree with me that white folks are still *not* listening and I know I'm tired of trying to communicate a relationship with them then, this relationship is over! It's just a matter of time you see, *before they come for me*! Question, how long do you think it will be before they come *again* for you too black America? Especially when they *rediscover* that there is no communication (or much too little) between black people and their relationships with each other! So let's talk and listen to one another in building stronger relationships that will never be over!

SPEND TO MEND THE BLACK COMMUNITY YOU LIVE IN

Say it isn't so. It is just to terrible to believe, much to sad, yet, it's also so true! My people (black people all over America) have bought into various false and negative beliefs about our own people, our inherent inferior talents and capabilities, and so-called racial weaknesses in the business and intellectual arenas of America, that more often than not—we practice a form of unconscious self-sabotage when it comes to building economical power (wealth) for our black-selves and collectively for our race here in America. A typical scenario—I've often visited suburban shopping malls to interview many of my sisters and brothers to find out why they continue to shop and spend their money in these mostly white retail-business enclaves.

Over the years, I've heard all kinds of lame, hypocritical, bullshit reasons and excuses, that all lend themselves to the obvious correct belief on my part that truly a lot of black people in America, definitely in Michigan, are indeed totally fucking brainwashed and seriously misguided. Many of these programmed brothers and sisters have absolutely no concept of what it means to Spend to mend the community they live in! Please someone, anyone, just tell me, what the hell is any real black man or woman supposed to think when he constantly hears shit like, "*well, I shop at this mall (store) because they sell only top quality merchandise, unlike similar stores within the city limits Oh, it's because I feel I get more for my money*" (another false perception.). "W*ell Brother Earl, I just like expensive and up-scale stores that carry name brand and designer labels, cause I know I'll like the feel and look when I get home*" (a brand name shirt or skirt is the same, regardless of who sells it or where its bought)! "*See here, the foods are better prepared, especially their meats, and the service is more friendly*" (an accepted snow job, for real), or the kids behind the counters, cashiers, bars and serving tables are better trained and more polite—this is debatable, and on and on.

"These people out here (white people) know how to treat you right," (keeping up with the white-Jones's is part of the problem, I'm sure). Of course, many white establishments and merchants will treat us like royalty, as long as they can take our precious dollars into their upscale neighborhoods and don't have to spend theirs in our communities!

I just want to scream right here! *"wake up my big-spending brothers and sisters, damn it! You are being had, and have been for many years!"* You are being seriously used, intentionally misled, and slowly economically destroyed by believing you're helping the greater good by spending your money in white populated areas! Answer this question please? How often is it that you see white suburbanites (en-masse or in large numbers like we do) driving into the inner-city to spend reams of cash, on anything like food, home and auto-services, or for merchandise of any kind, medical services, banking, etc., (unless it's a very popular annual downtown warehouse sale or such)? Yet we all know that white folks make the trip downtown (after dark usually) to purchase sex, drugs, and hot auto-parts, as well as to gamble and raise all sorts of hell! But hardly to spend their riches without giving much thought to what effect it will have on the city proper (and its black inhabitants) or with black merchants! It's a fact that we know is true, because we can still see it happening!

Black people, especially black women, truly need to investigate how to spend to mend the black communities they live in. We need to understand the myth and the hidden message that *"white people can be trusted over our own people, and white businesses are better than black businesses"* is truly economical suicide! It's all a great big lie! A hocus-pocus, debilitating, money grabbing, Madison Avenue magician's trick, used to legally rob black people blind which has been hammered into the thick skulls of black folks for years to keep our dollars flowing into their hands and out of our own, so as to keep us in-debt and beholding to white American capitalists and other ethnic robber-barons. The very game of commercialism and so-called free-enterprise as it exists, manages to keep black cities and communities impoverished and economically dependent on white businesses and merchants! We black folks (I venture the majority and especially our young non-discriminating black spenders and buyers) truly need to wake up to this serious reality, this self-perpetuating monetary deceit! It is this—*"anything made by or sold by white people is inherently of better quality, cheaper in price, longer-lasting, will lift us up, make our day, ease more of our pain, turn us on quicker, make us more acceptable to our peers, make us more beautiful (euro-centric), give us more free time, will be less filling and still taste great, and on and on!"*

When black people bite (the way we do and have for years) hard into this type of psychological addicting bullshit, we inevitably end up as co-conspirators in our own impoverishment! We become the new robber-barons, merchant-crooks, slum lords, and blood sucking wealth leaches of our own communities! Everyday, every time we spend our disposable incomes outside of our own neighborhoods and communities, we slowly kill off the good life, the economical and psychological benefits (not to mention racial respect) that automatically accrues to an area that invests in itself. Our mutual prosperity is directly tied into our mutual financial support of one another. Why can't black people see this simple fact for what it is—black survival? Blacks investing in themselves and each other equals economical power for us all!

Just look at our recent history here in America. Take just the last 120 years. The pattern has been shown to us again and again, the road made clear. Each and every other race or nationality that immigrates to America has followed the same example as the white pioneers. Find new land (real-estate has eternal value for obvious reasons), conquer the land (remove the natives to less productive areas), work the land, build on it, grow something to sell, then, rent the left-over out to the less fortunate for generations to come! Also, help the Italians become merchants and slum lords, then rich and powerful, do the same for the Jews, then again for the Chinese, Japanese, Koreans, next the Arabs, Chaldeans, Indians (from India), and last but not least—give the plan for wealth that works so well (and for some reason remains hidden to black people) to the southern white lower class, so the cycle of producing real wealth in America can start all over again <u>without</u> the inclusion of blacks. Somebody tell me please, why is it so damn hard for us (educated American blacks) to see that which is constantly staring us in our faces? "*If you black folks don't shop where you live, you can't live for long where you don't shop.*" We <u>must</u> spend (shop) to mend the communities we live in!

White wealth in America today comes primarily from whites spending and sharing their earned incomes within the predominately white areas they live and work in. Their dollars circulates between them (the butcher, the baker, the candle-stick maker) in their communities from eight to twelve days on average thereby enriching themselves and their communities, while blacks shopping in those areas are perceived as big, bonus dollars! That helps to support and maintain white's high standard of life and living! The little money that black people do spend in the hood, has a circulation life of only three to four days (as reported in the great black book by Dr. Claude Anderson—<u>Black Labor/White Wealth</u>) before it becomes lost to the black community forever. My people, this shit has got to stop, if we ever hope to reverse the game results of collective wealth-building in America, so as to benefit more black people and our communities.

Now please pay attention here, especially you young up and coming black professionals, and twenty-first century black middle-class buyers and spenders. Almost everything you can buy outside of your own communities, now-a-days, can be found somewhere in your community! Also, in truth, there are <u>no real differences</u> in quality, freshness, durability, taste, services or merchandise, between the inner-city and similar sources within the suburbs! The few cents more you pay for local goods and services is solely due to a slightly higher cost of doing business in black areas (as controlled by white banks, insurance carriers, and often local government agencies), because they wish to keep the business status-quo as is because it benefits them and their special interests, but not black families and their communities! If you could ask those in the know why this is—you often won't get the truth, because these things (cost of doing business, red-tape, licensing, capital requirements, etc.) are tools used by the system to keep the monies flowing in the "*right direction*", in the direction of building wealth for whites and their progeny. To take the gold of the black neighborhoods into their care and safekeeping so that they can continue to rule over all others; haven't we heard this often enough? They who control the gold makes all the rules for the rest of us to follow? So there's no need to really practice the golden rule of sharing and treating all others as equals as long as we remain asleep to the true meaning of white-surburban greed! Blacks had better research and apply the uplifting and self-empowering principles of unity and entrepreneurship, again, as it applies to our own dreams and aspirations for our future survival and that of our progeny as we move even closer to a truly world economy! We need to embrace with all our collective strength, the attitude of spending for the mending of the communities we live in. We need to become aware (again studying black history) of our rich past and the many examples of our own self-sufficiency and real independence, when white businesses chose not to serve us because of racism and their thought that there was no profits to be gained by doing so.

Now-a-days companies like Hudsons and Pier-One keep and maintain large in-store black merchandise areas, to cater to and profit off the newer black attitudes and African pride of some of our people. I've always wondered just what my black brothers and sisters (not too long ago) of Boleo Oklahoma and places like Rosewood Texas and even Detroit's Black Bottom 50-60 years ago knew that blacks today seem not to know about building and running their own businesses for the benefit and enrichment of our people collectively. Many did it then and were quite successful, and entire black cities like Boleo, Oklahoma and Rosewood (black Wallstreet) Texas prospered until whites came knocking for the land! White's greed and racism is money and land motivated. Always has been, and will continue to be!

It is all too clear to me and must become clear to my people—if we ever hope to become truly equal and free, and financially independent in America, we must begin at once to collectively shop and spend with black merchants and black businesses within our own neighborhoods and communities—at least for one or two expensive items. If we truly wish not to become even more dependent on white folks selling us needed goods and services in 2000 and beyond. Black businesses and aspiring young black entrepreneurs know all too well today, what they must do and how hard they must work just to change the negative mindset of many blacks. Again, for example, "*It has never been true that one or two bad apples on the tree has spoiled all the rest of the apples*" (in the black business world). We must continue to strive to overcome our self-perpetuating inferior business perceptions and renew our faith in our own true abilities to service, buy and sell from one another!

We must collectively pledge to once again trust and support black businesses, movies, books, media, music (including some rap artists), also black trade-unions, black Masonic lodges, Shriners, black banks, and all those black enterprises that are trying to uplift the black race here in America, especially certified black charities, and social-aid organizations like inner-city drug treatment and education programs. We have the money to do it! Our combined annual disposable income exceeds 300-billion dollars each year! We must spend some of this money to mend the black communities we live in, if we hope to live at all in a decent and respected environment here in America's urban jungles and fertile south-lands. When we begin to do these things on a regular basis, then many black businesses will surely come to realize as white businesses already do, that the money is the honey—that enriches the bees, that satisfies the needs of the hives (community).

To my people, let us pledge today to allow our dollars to make a difference in the areas in which we live and worship. Let us shop black, save often, and spend to mend the communities we live in! Let us do this for our precious old people and our valuable children. Those beautiful blacks who will suffer the most, if we don't prepare to take care of them while we still can. I predict that we all will one day need each other (black people) sooner than we think! Keep an eye on the white militia movement and the stock market. Can we ever become 65-70 million united and wealthy blacks? I do believe over time we can—we must, we will! Excuse me,

I think I feel an itch, and if I don't scratch it—who will? True power to the people and for our people—starts with the almighty dollar, know it!

From Professor Amos N. Wilson's book Black on Black Violence (p.153). (dreams with means). "*How can a community which spends only five cents out of every dollar it earns with itself; which spends approximately 300 billion dollars with those who exploit it; 300 billion dollars which support the desires, lifestyles and standards of living of other ethnic groups while dis-investing in its own children not encourage criminality and violence within its confines, while attenuating criminality and violence in those communities it so thoughtlessly subsidizes. When the black community squanders the economic inheritance of its own children for those of other communities, when it does not reevaluate its consummatory behavior in terms of its long-term interests—it gets the crime it deserves*" Oh, so we can take a big bite out of crime in the black community and at the same time we can increase our economical power (wealth) in America. If more of us would just do what we all know we should! "*spend to mend the black communities we live in*"... it's so simple-so damn simple! We don't need white people's permission to spend our dollars at home where we live and work! We need to stop acting white (supporting whites), start acting black again, taking care of our race, and hold accountable (and punish—boycott) those few bourgeois, greedy, selfish blacks that refuse to cooperate for the good of us all! I don't care how many new T.V commercials aimed at black people by Denny's Corporation I see. Even though they have settled multiple discrimination cases with blacks, I will never spend a dollar within a Denny's restaurant for the rest of my life. Discrimination hurts black people everywhere and reaffirms why we should eat more and spend more at Yusef's place. He never had a problem serving soul food to black people—as long as they didn't ask for credit... spend to mend! Bet!

NO RESPECT FOR MY SECURITY

Tis a cruel and inhuman world in which I live –
I've found no respect for the paid-in-full security I give.

By day or by night, I stand or walk for hours on end –
By day and especially on lonely nights, I cannot find a friend.

As I speak, yes I am spoken to often in unkind tones of voice–Refusing to be afraid or unemployed, I never have much choice.

This then is my thankless plight, no real fault of my mind –
I beg no special indulgence, just try and understand my kind.

I've found fulfillment in a spiritual way, doing the work I do–
Enough is earned to feed and clothe me, but not enough for two.

My brothers of the Law hold me in contempt, I often wonder why –
Some treat me with occasional malice and say my security is a lie.

Still, I take pride in doing a job no one else really wants –
One day I'll find a friend while working-guarding the public's haunts.

My son wiped an unconscious tear from my eye and asked,
"Daddy, why is your job so hard?"
I smiled and slowly replied, "Son I guess it's false pride.
You see, daddy's a security guard" … . .

So let us show them a little more respect, will you?
If you think about it – They truly deserve it!
Again, especially if they are black!

BLACK PEOPLE AND A.D.D.

Everybody black knows at least one or two adults who, for whatever reason was not diagnosed as kids with Attention Deficit Disorder, and should have been. Those individuals amongst us who can't concentrate, stay focused, or remember yesterday. Who just can't pay attention to save their life! Have you heard of Attention Deficit Disorder? It appears to be affecting (or infecting) many of our kids these days, as well as many adult persons in the black community. Some to greater or lesser degrees, it's obvious to me now-a-days, that there was no earlier childhood intervention for some of my black brothers and sisters around the country. How is it that some black folks can live and move within a country and not know where they're at, why they're here, where they are going, or where they came from (no awareness of their roots). It's said by today's physicians that, if A.D.D. is not diagnosed and treated with drugs early on, it can and will later on permanently negatively impact on a child, especially when that child becomes an adult and need to think as an adult.

Well for those of us who are blessed to be in what appears as full possession of our mental faculties, we now know why some of our people are the way they are: slow and helpless, and at the mercy of the mind and body manipulators among our own people, not to mention their love for and support of white society's quest to keep us all distracted, separated, distrusting of one another, and fearful of our own future success as a united people in body, mind and spirit! Some of our truest enemies today, are some of our own people who have sold their very souls to white America, and have no qualms about turning their yellow backs, or actually, willingly participating in America's continued oppression of their own race! Shit, I often wonder when and where A.D.D. got it's start in our people. I suspect that black people will never know the true answer to this question, whether it's due to genetics, as we are accustomed to being told, or have we been secretly exposed to some new drug or chemical that

America's white scientists needed to test on a particular group of people? Like black people, etc., white South African scientist freely admitted they had similar plans and viral poisons for their rebellious natives during the truth commission hearings in 1998. No one asked them the current location of their nefarious formulas I recall.

Now for those of us who are truly capable of paying attention, let us ponder this possible answer to the origins of mysterious diseases like A.D.D. affecting some of our people. Take as an example the popular widespread system of treating our water supplies around the country these days, where the water is treated with flavor enhancing chemicals and specific cleaning processes that are supposed to protect and in some cases nourish us (those who depend upon these supplies for drinking water). Take the chemical additive fluoride, fluoridation of drinking water. Contrary to what we may have been led to believe, fluoride and some of it's derivatives and in chemical combinations (like with chlorine) not only harms our health, but in certain amounts and combinations with other chemicals can actually be used as an effective tool for mind-control! I asked an elder long-term black chemical engineer to confirm this, pleading with him to be straight with me, because a mind is a terrible thing to abuse in any manner, and he did! He also exclaimed like most undercover, back door "*Negro stoolies*", Now you can't quote me on this, if you promise not to use my name, I'll be willing to tell you something else you probably didn't know. Oh hell yeah, I promised and promised on one knee, I begged him to tell me more! He said: that he had actually seen old files some years ago while working for a large Midwestern water treatment facility, marked in red letters "**SENSITIVE/CONFIDENTIAL**." He said he opened it and read that the Germans during World War II, had successfully used fluorides as a means of mind and population control! Did I hear him correctly? Oh hell yeah, we were talking mind-control! He said that "*they (the Germans) had discovered that after one year of a person consuming fluoride-laced water, something occurred in their brains which made them very docile and more easily managed.*" Damn, he interjected, that he was shocked as hell! I asked my elder brother if he thought this was done to the Jewish prisoners in those German concentration camps. Could this explain why so many of them stood by and passively allowed their families to be shipped off to God only knows where, or for what evil intent? Yet they continued to believe that all would be well! He said Hell, he wouldn't know anything about that, and he was just relating back to me what he had actually seen with his own eyes He said that *"the file went on to say the Soviets had done studies that showed fluorides were extremely important in introducing a docile, sheep-like, obedience in the general population."*

Question to all intelligent black people of today: Could fluoridated water used extensively around America now-a-days be used for this same sinister purpose? This brother engineer then stated that, "the file then went on to say that the earlier fluorides were administered in a person's life, the quicker the cumulative effects will take hold and last longer." I then remembered that back in the early 1980s, a fluoride product called Swish, was introduced into the public market place, touting it's cavity prevention effects or something of the sort. I also thought to myself that today, damn, nearly all dental products and especially toothpaste all contain fluoride! Not a day goes by where I don't wonder if this brother was telling me the truth, or just trying to appear blacker than most highly educated Negroes. Still, I found it strangely peculiar that six or seven months later, I couldn't find this helpful brother at this fairly new chemical company in the hood, where he said he had been working for three years. They told me he had one day just disappeared, left town, vanished without leaving a forwarding address. Sure? The last thing he had told me was that I needed to read a book called Matrix-III: The Psycho, Social, Chemical, Biological and Electronic Manipulation of Human Consciousness, by Valdamar Valerian (I'm not sure of the spelling)... I'm still trying to locate the book, and wonder if that was his true source for what he had shared with me seven months earlier. One day I'll know the truth. I'll find that book!

I can't put my finger on it, or on just what it was or even when it happened. But, I refuse to believe a great black race that was once so powerful and civilized like those old African nations (empires) of Songhay, Mali, and Greater Ghana and Egypt, could give off a people, like black folks of today, who can so easily accept the contemporary, mentally lingering, negative effects of past enslavement, and self-destructive social manipulations by a white power elite in America. Like continued white racism, discrimination, automatic weapons and poisonous drugs continuing to exist within our own neighborhoods and communities today! I truly believe at some point in time—past or present, during our stay here in America, controlling and ruthless whites planned and executed more than the infamous Tuskegee syphilis experiment on black people. How many of us remember the civil unrest and detention plans our government drew up during and shortly after the many urban riots of the late sixties, following years of peaceful non-violent protest and marches for equal rights by blacks in America? Fact: Our government drew up real plans to lock up black Americans enmass if the riots and burning had continued. You will be utterly surprised by what you can get nowa-days via the Freedom of Information Act, if you know what to ask for, and where to look! This just may explain why many of the majority of American blacks are perceived of as being so passive, docile (law-abiding), and non-threatening in spite of America's continued abuses toward her own and the world's people of color. It's truly sad that most black people still can't see the big bad white wolf (for what he really is) living right next door to us. The new black-sheep in our newly integrated suburban communities, primarily because we feel we have arrived somewhere special, after fighting and struggling so hard to get there. Question: have blacks truly arrived at first-class citizenship status here in America, or is it just that many blacks today falsely believe that they can and do, enjoy true freedom even though more than two-thirds of their black and brown brothers are still mentally and physically enslaved all across America! Isn't it possible that these upwardly mobile blacks may have been misdiagnosed as kids, and still suffer from Attention Deficit Disorder? I will always maintain that no man is ever truly free as long as his brothers and sisters of the same race (black and human) are held in bondage, mentally, spiritually, or physically!

I predict that if we (black Americans) continue to fail to pay attention to what's really coming down around America's current people politics (the growth of white militias and neo-Nazi hate groups, etc.), and the continued experimentation with chemical and technological social manipulation of people's minds. America will begin a quick slide into social chaos and decline. It is quite possible that my people (black people) will wake up one day to shockingly discover that their breakfast—grits or oatmeal, has been replaced with solent-green (or solent-black—ground up black body parts) served to them for breakfast, lunch, and dinner on the new federal black reservations in America, circa 2010 A.F.D.D. I often wondered how many of my fellow blacks have noticed or experienced a sudden loud, yet short, temporary ringing in their ears lately, causing them to sit up or at least look up into space, and then it fades as quickly as it came. Do we honestly know how far subliminal seduction (or subliminal destruction) via satellite technology has come in the last 25 years? Why do I ask this serious question? Go rent the movie <u>Enemy of the State</u> starring Will Smith. Subliminally, (subconsciously) again and again, <u>a black man</u> is portrayed as the deadly enemy of the state (the U.S.A). Didn't a white man (Gene Hackman) in the movie tell us of some of the awful shit that government satellites could do to a motherfucker. Pay attention black America - our freedom is not free! do you feel me my people, do you? Again, everybody knows at least one or two black adults who, for whatever reason, was not diagnosed as kids with A.D.D. Maybe they didn't have this debilitating disease as a child, but only recently received it, subliminally? Damn, I'm afraid to turn on my television or computer now-a-days for fear either one may suddenly tell me where to report—"*after the fires, death and destruction*!" (A.F.D.D.). Thank God I stopped drinking tap water and brushing my teeth with fluoride-laced toothpaste years ago? Now I wonder what I, and my people, must do to survive America's current people politics and the current high-ass prices of that other white meat (ground turkey)! Yo, white America, please don't fuck with my chicken. Right, right! I known damn well I won't eat no "*solent-black*" no matter who serves it up! Damn that A.D.D!

TO BE OR NOT TO BE—STEREOTYPED

For those of us who are black (Afro-American/Colored) American citizens who are consciously awake (of which I am honored to be). I know damn well I am not alone in stating, shouting even, or just plain-old screaming this out. I am tired of other people and a few of my own, typecasting, labeling, or stereotyping me, my race, my heritage, my culture! For too many of my people, there is a daily choice to make upon rising each and every morning. It is to be or not to be a stereotype… to accept or not to accept, someone else's concept/perception of who we are. How difficult this process must be for many of my people. For me the choice has always been easy. I choose to be what my God made me, I choose to be a beautiful black human being—Period!

Not colored and crazy —not a black man and lazy
Not brown and sad—not violent and bad
Not dark-skinned with nappy head—not hyper-sexed with a sin-filled bed.
Not black to be held back—not brown and permitted to stand around.
Not vicious and destructive bent on destroying our town.
Not a pseudo-white—to be seen as a child of the light.
Not a tan, or bronze, or colored boogie man.
Not a nigger descendent from the nigger motherland.
Not just a black always asking upper-crust society for slack.
Not light or coco brown—to be a regular target of the beat down.
Not mentally deranged or emotionally confused, walking around with a constant frown.
Not a suntanned light almost white—to be associated with all that's right.
Not just a nice educated colored person—to be lean and seen, never mean.
I choose to be what my God has made me—just a great black human-being.

"IT IS ENOUGH!"

THOSE PERPETRATING NEGROES

Word up! Plenty of shouts (or screams) gotta go out to all of my brothers and sisters still carrying those Neimus Marcus and Saks Filth Avenue shopping bags. You know the ones with the big-ass holes in the side and the frayed handles. What's up with some of ya'll wearing those expensive Gucci, Donna Karan, Perry Ellis two-piece outfits, with those grease-stained collars and sleeves around the wrists? Give me a damn break will you? On those fake-ass Rolex watches and Versace diamond tennis bracelets you purchased at the local corner gas station and not at a reputable jewelry store (in white areas , gas stations sell only gas and oil, tobacco and pop). So please my people, stop this material madness, just be yourselves and live within your means. Please stop this sickening and obvious perpetration! Will you take some time to count the many blessings you already have, that didn't cost you a damn dime (like sunshine and trees- fresh air and bees). Please brothers and sisters, get the hell out of those lycra/spandex bicycle pants, and tiny-ass T-shirts that will barely fit the bodies of your little kids! Can we please give away or throw out those expensive K-Swiss, Adidas, and Air-Jordan gym shoes that you all paid too damn much for when they were new and all white and now you're still wearing them everywhere, even though they're now all black and gray! Damn! Stop it! Just stop it please!

I do declare, the shit that perpetrating niggers everyday will try and get away with! Need I mention those used/new Navigators and Expeditions that some of you drive with such pride that still belong to the finance companies, credit unions/banks? You should not be parking them in back alleys, cause ya'll can't afford a decent house with a driveway, that's a dead-ass giveaway. Oh hell yes, hang up those cellular phones that you know have expired long ago, and don't be ashamed to cash in your two or three beepers with the dead batteries—cause you know absolutely nobody is trying to reach you, and you know this! Dig this real shit here, whenever we fake the funk, life has a way of exposing us as the simple materialists that many of us have become! Never realizing the old truth, "*You can fool some of the people some of the time, but you can't fool all of the people all of the time!*" Whenever we come to value our self-worth based on our acquired material assets/possessions, we inevitably become a slave to things. Know this my perpetuating friends, to become a slave to anything or anyone is to debase the life-sustaining natural gifts and freedom God has given each and everyone of us! God hasn't made anything (or anyone) that can be called junk! But man has made plenty.

OK, Ok, sister, is that really your hair, of course it is, cause you bought it only yesterday! Girl, are those really your nails? I don't think so, cause every hussy's fingernails on the block (on the job) is the exact same length and style. My brother, please, one earring is enough ok, and that body piercing, won't work any better than some serious exercise at attracting members of the opposite sex!

Oh my Lord—What are we going to do with all these perpetrating Negroes? I know what I would like to do with all of them, but it's against the white man's laws for now!

Look over there, there goes one, here comes one now! Oh hell yes, they know who they are! Oh, so you got a college degree and still can't pump your own gas, or know how to tie you shoes—damn! How sad! Hey Cleopatra—please allow me to do the cooking in my kitchen. I know perpetrating negroes don't cook! But will support Colonel Sanders! And Mr. Remy Marten.

BLACK PEOPLE AND COMPUTERS

Help! Question: If you are black, and you should know if you are (because white-assed America knows and won't let you/us forget it). Answer these simple questions for me, please? What is a computer? OK. What are computers used for? Now what do you know about computers and the hundreds of software programs that instructs computers? Well, just what good is computer knowledge anyway? Oh, so you answered, you don't know anything about computers and could care even less! You say you've managed all these years without the little monster! Check this shit out—if I could I surely would, take me an razor strap to that ass, or asses! Why? I'm so glad you asked!

First, sometimes a good spanking is called for. Secondly, the future is calling, and old white-ass corporate America only want to hear from those individuals with some computer skills… period! If you are black, and you should know if you are, and care nothing about computers, you'd better read this next line of text at least 100 times and come to understand what it conveys! *"That is exactly what America of the 21st century will care about you— nothing, nothing, nothing!"* You won't be able to earn a living, nor receive cable, radio, video, public-broadcast T.V. or manage your home, your money, your life.

Without computer assistance, you won't have access to Internet information, web-sites, education and services, nor any electronic control over your own privacy, health, or voting rights! I was privy to hear a black middle-class, educated couple complain to a store clerk—how much trouble they were having trying to motivate their 10 and 12 year olds to read and write well. So they were shopping for an expensive video game system (with $300.00 worth of action-packed games) to use as leverage. I said, excuse me my people, have you ever tried an inexpensive extension cord on their naked bottoms? You would have thought I said something about their mothers, the way they looked at me! I know that both of them earned over $50,000 a piece per year (the clerk told me later that they had told her earlier) yet they felt they couldn't afford a computer for their spoiled and lazy kids!

If you're black, and you should know if you are—you and your kids must know something, something, something about computers! Black people's very survival may well depend on it! I doubt if video games skills qualify! Believe it! A computer is a must have!

Black parents need to be reminded—the white baby doctor, Dr. Spock—had admitted he may have been mistaken back in 1974 about the harm of spanking your children. In too many black homes these days, it's hard to tell who the parents are and who are the kids. Since the kids dictate to and often spank the parents! No child under 16 should be allowed to rule a home without first knowing how to rule a computer and hold down a damn job! Case closed. Period! Instead of a damn Sony Playstation this Christmas for little Mustafa and Mendi get them a damn computer. Even a used machine is better than no computer at all. For motivating your kids, invest in a little tuff love, you know the kind, go ask your grandmother!

BLACK PEOPLE AND COMPUTERS, PART II

It's true, just the other day, I observed in the metro section of our newspaper (here in Motown), A national white supremist group founded by former Klu-Klux-Klan leader, David Duke, is trying to establish new group chapters in and around many big U.S. cities via the Internet (on-line computer communications) to recruit new members to their cause! Damn! The article went on to say: The "*(N.A.A.W.P.) National Association of White People officials say that their group is not a racist organization, but current information from their web-site indicates otherwise! An example (naive Negroes better pay attention here)", "Increased minority crime is destroying the social fabric of America.*" Their web-site reads, "*high illegitimate minority birth-rates, if allowed to continue will one day make them (black folks, I guess) the majority and give them political control of our country.*" I don't think so, we're too far from being a united majority like whites are in this country to be considered a serious threat to anybody! "*Like they have already done in large black cities—taken control*!" In the same article, a Mr. D. Cohen, Executive Director of the Anti-Defamation League of Michigan stated, "We're getting the word out to local residents (a warning) in these areas, to be on their guard against these computer recruiting tactics. This just might be the way to keep them out. I think the best thing for people to do is simply to ignore them." Yeah, Mr. Cohen, right. Just keep on ignoring them! Well I decided to go on-line to see for myself just what the hell the Klan, oops, I mean the N.A.A.W.P. was trying to sell unsuspecting white folks, in and around the metropolitan suburbs of major cities. Black folks had better get computer literate real fast, the shit you can find on the Internet is truly unbelievable! Just looking up some of the Internet web-links to the N.A.A.W.P.s web-site, will take your ass to some of the vilest neo-Nazi and white hate groups in the country! Oh yes, Mr. Cohen also stated, "*There is something going on out there.*" No shit! I couldn't find any hate or racist propaganda on the net from the N.A.A.C.P. (the National Association of the Advancement of Colored People). Maybe this is one reason, we (colored folks) and the N.A.A.C.P. are not as well armed or as violent as these other computerized groups! Then again, maybe I'm just a worry-wart and worry too much, since our government's police agencies (and a lot of young black people) don't seem to be too concerned! Only until it becomes too late, and another tragedy has struck the black community somewhere in America. Well, here I go again for my people, those with guns keep them close, and never trade your weapons for cheese (cash) or anything else; you may need them most when you least expect it. I'm also very curious about things "ambiguous" (coming from our government). I wonder how many of my people today, actually believe that our president is serious about addressing the "race issue" in America these days! A president who has yet to order Ms. Janet Reno to sick the dogs on all those white, Aryian Nation type organizations they know of hoarding tons of illegal guns and explosives (for what?) and they know where they hang out! Those neo-Nazi and Klan groups that continue to plan the killings of blacks, Jews, and homosexuals in our midst! One must kill, often as an initiation into these groups.

How many more federal buildings need to be blown up, or how many more innocent black couples (holding hands, strolling down the street minding their own business) must be shot in the face, so that a white soldier within the U.S. Army and the Aryian army can earn his black-spider web tattoo? How many more times must these heinous crimes be reported before the C.I.A. or F.B.I. get involved to protect the lives of the Black people, Jewish people, and homosexual Americans? The organization "Klan-Watch" (bless their hearts) has recently reported that approximately 49 murders (that they know of) have been committed by skin-heads around the country since 1988 (statistics and polls) and that there are allegedly only 4,000 skin-heads in the U.S.A. (bullshit!). How many are there with hair?) Damn, have we (black folks) forgotten what it feels like to be caught off guard (pants down, ass out), unprepared for the unthinkable, that becomes the thinkable daily in the news? What will it take for us to stand up and ask the President, "when will our government or local law enforcement begin to protect us black folks" because we are still unable to (or unwilling) to protect ourselves, from white racist hate groups (blacks that are currently on-line should check-out the net-links from the N.A.A.W.P. web-site that leads out to the Eilohim-City web-site where they advertise to teach and train whites only (how to build truck-bombs, toss hand-grenades, and fire the latest automatic weapons for a fee!) and neo-Nazi skinheads that are hell-bent on harming unsuspecting and unthreatening Black Americans!?

I honestly left my computer-search and silently wondered if this real "*war on the Internet*" would ever empty out of my computer and into the streets of urban black and rural America? To my peace loving people, if you are black, and you should know if you are, you must know something about computers! Video-game skills won't qualify! So drop the NFL-98/NBA-JAM, and go take a gun-safety/shooting class instead! After that, go buy a computer, if you don't already own one, and learn how to pull the trigger (turn it on) on line-in time. Peace.

GHETTO, GHETTO

Ghetto – (noun) Ghet-tos or ghet-toes: some still call it the slums-—a part of a city in which members of a minority group live.

I hear lately that the word ghetto is becoming popular again, among young blacks and whites this year! Even on radio and T.V. *"He's so ghetto, and oh girl, she's very ghettoish, and they live in the ghett-toe!—You don't want to go down there." Question—just what the fuck is up with this new shit?* Black folks better ask somebody! Why is it our inferior, crime-ridden, run-down cities are experiencing a white influx and rebirth, while the suburbs (where we were once not allowed to live) are becoming the new black ghettos? Is it because many upwardly mobile blacks live their lives being the black-shadows of prosperous –nomadic white people? If so, save the expense of moving again. Stay your black asses right where you're at—in the cities ghetto! Look around, white people are coming back! Suckers—Bet! Question: "which is more valuable to you during a race riot? (coming to a suburban neighborhood near you real soon) a home in the ghet'toe or a expensive home in a white surburb? Where you are surrounded by the enemy. Think about it—the world is a ghetto? So where are you moving to when you leave the world?

I just want to scream right here! Wake up my big-spending brothers and sisters—Damn! America is still the home of the weak and the land of the slave, regardless of how much your house cost you! Ghetto—(noun) for too many blacks, a mental vision of a driveway, white picket fence, 2-car garage and pissed off white neighbors—Damn!

SISTERS BETTER WAKE UP

Oh yes it's true, my black sisters had better wake up! Because you see, white women want them a black man bad. Asian women want them a black man, Mexican women want them a black man too, while Arab women want them one also, as well as West-Indian women, and South American women, and American liberated women, and rich women, and lonely women, and other women not of color, just to be able to say they got them a big, strong, sexy black buck! So sisters better come correct, or they may not come at all. These many hungry and horny women can't all be wrong (or are these women a part of a greater conspiracy?) It's true, some brothers are getting laid and paid! Many of the above ladies will pay for a blackman! Just like they did during slavery!

There were nearly 1.3 million married interracial couples in 1994, the U.S. Census Bureau reported, four times the number in 1970! Damn—what up with this shit? This quiet storm on the horizon. Sisters better wake up! Too many brothers are still asleep! "*Keeping in mind there are two types of love jails—one for whorish brothers, the other for my sisters still waiting to exhale.*" With practice—we can come together again. Bet!

A small bit of necessary advice to those player brothers (pseudo pimps) who think they can continue to cross racial boarders to sink their faces into an occasional white bowl for a quickie and some "*chump change*", then creep back across the tracks to some black sister's bed—better wise up, many black women today are perceptive, intelligent and discerning, and absolutely refuse to get their swerve on with a brother with white milk on his mustache when chocolate milk is just as wholesome and attractive! Personally, I prefer chocolate ladies who prefer chocolate man. Again, with practice we can come together.

P.S. Right now, today! Brothers and sisters need to read a great new book on black male and female relationships by Debben Millner, (Titled: Sister Rules How to Get a Good Black Man and Keep Him). Also, How to Love a Black Woman by Dr. Ronn Elmore, author of How to Love a Black Man – Bet!

THE LADIES BATHROOMS

Well now, here's a timely message to the ladies, oops, I mean to some of my little sisters. Dig this, some of you should be more aware of the fact that bathrooms and comfort-stops at work and other public locales, are becoming increasingly unisex facilities (whatever this may imply). And some of you need to be reminded to clean up after your visits to the bath/toilet/restroom, damn it! Why? Oh you've got the nerve to ask? OK—ask any honest, hard working female custodian, which of the bathrooms are the cleanest at the end of the workday? Listen to her horror stories! Wanna bet they will all agree it's the men's that's the cleanest? Shame on all you "*Nice Nasty Girls*" and you know who you are! I know your mothers raised you all better than this, so pick up after yourselves, and don't forget to wash your hands! You'll never know when a custodian (or a man) may come in after you leave out! OK? Shameful, just shameful, and we know this! There is no acceptable excuse for squalor, especially in a kitchen or bathroom—at home or at work... believe it ladies! Fellas..hope you are paying attention. Whenever you all unzip your pants and urinate in public, somebody always sees your vulgar behavior, even at night. Real potty-training was missed by a few of my brothers and sisters, and its still a damn shame and we know this! Excuse me—what's that smell! Don't tell me because I already know!—Damn shame!

LITTLE BLACK CINDERELLA

Question: How far have we (black folk) come in America as a people, as a wise and enlightened race! Just what have black people become or have turned into lately? Recently on a national televised court show, I observed an attractive well-built Creole-looking (red-bone/high yellow) sister, who was being sued by her 62 year-old ex-boyfriend a self-professed "sugar daddy" who just happened to be a white man! He proudly stated to the judge, that they had an arrangement, that she has refused to honor now, because she wanted to end the relationship and see other boys. She stated to the judge that they had only entered into that arrangement three years earlier because she was down on her luck and needed some money fast!

For three years, this young sister was willing to sell herself, her body, and sexual favors (while actually living with a white "*Chester-the-Child Molester*") for a measly few thousand dollars and a good used car! Damn! As I sat and watched the proceedings, I asked myself—as did the white female judge (after she bitterly scolded the old dude for having an affair with an 18-year old person—who is now 21—and I agreed), "*You, young lady, are still a baby, you haven't lived long enough to even know your own body, least of all what to do for somebody else's, even for pay! It is called prostitution girlfriend*!" She went on to say (as my sister held her nose high), "*I don't know what your mama taught you, or failed to teach you, because you should never sell yourself, regardless of what you wish to call it, for money! You as a beautiful person, are truly worth more than that! Where is your pride, your self-respect, your dignity?*" The judge ended her lecture by saying, "*the only person you, young lady, was tricking, getting over on (getting paid on her back) was yourself*!" Damn, I thought, yeah judge, tell her fine ass off. I too, wonder what her mother and father failed to teach her about black pride, about white people, and white men in particular, or about the history of black people living here in America. Hell, I even wondered when the judge ordered my young sister (it was a civil trial for small claims to be settled), to pay back the old dapper white man (the cost of her used car), whether or not she felt any shame during this very public exposure. Oh yeah, I indeed wondered, just what have we come to as black people living in America, when our children and young people see no harm or danger in prostituting themselves by sleeping with and living with white folks!

I truly believe that as black parents, some where in our recent history, we collectively have failed our progeny! Is money truthfully the end all to be all? If so, we'd better (collectively) prepare to once again live with the white man's perverted sexual greed and his evil intentional manipulation of our race and our young inexperienced children who seek a few dollars more, or perhaps—a glass slipper! Poor little Black Cinderella! She thought she was slick... she never got to meet Dapper Dan's mother! I wonder why not? Many blacks contend that white men today and in American history has always had their way with black females. I say it takes two to tangle, (like O.J. and Clarence Thomas) and maybe black women and black men are entitled to make a few mistakes. Besides, whoever claimed all Prince Charmings are always white? White folks still do, so don't believe it! I personally know of no less than six dapper black Prince Charmings in my hood over 45 who would gladly finance an 18 or 20 year old black Cinderella's dreams as long as she was not schizophrenic, too macho, or extremely greedy. All young black Cinderellas need to be reminded—a sugar daddy is only a "*John*" (or trick) and any sister serving up sex for money is just a damn prostitute! Believe it! More self-love and self-respect is all they need!

OPRAH

Oh how I would love to see our very own Ms. Winfrey do more of her shows on black people and our adopted western life style here in America (keep it black girlfriend, a few more brown faces in your audience won't hurt your ratings either). I've found a ton of strange and wonderful black stories she could showcase, right here on my block in the hood. Like how this young brother, just two doors down from me can afford a 1998 Yukon and a freshly detailed '76 SS-Chevy Super Sport, several cellular phones, three or four fully loaded automatic weapons, the biggest (and loudest) stereo-system in Detroit and every hook-up (Fresh Gear clothing) is draped with gold jewelry. All without having a job at 25 or 26-years old. OK—here's a thought, (rumors abound in the hood), God forbid Ms. Winfrey ever chooses a rich white man for a husband over brother Stedman, money isn't everything is it? Hell, I wouldn't know, maybe I'll ask my young neighbor—a real O.G. (old style gangster) down the street. I-Aahhiiee don't think so… got some sweet advice for my bigger brother Stedman though (based on speculations in the hood)—You gotta be a "*Stud man*", my brother, please don't let us poorer brothers (financially, not physically)down. Hey, what-the-fuck? The headlines might one day read "*Stedman is gay and color struck*". Oh no! Where on earth is Spike Lee when we need him? Damn! If I ever get a chance to put my lips on that fine thick woman, I'll tickle her belly button from the inside. "Hey O-prah, much love and respect for ya. Big Earl dreams big dreams OK. I love your eyes and them thighs—love me some hips and lips too! So keep it black woman, if you want me watching! Peace. My beloved.

SOME WOMEN AND THEIR PETS

Lordy, lordy, big brother Earl, why you wanna put our business in the street, why you serve us up like this? Check this my sisters; let me break you off a little something, something. Many of you already know what big mouths you have, like big-ass water buckets with a big hole in the bottom. You can't keep water (your business) in it if you were dying of thirst, because you're too busy dying to tell someone-anybody! Besides, Big Earl is cut like this, to truly know me is to love me! So talk to the hand, I ain't trying to debate with you right now, check this shit out—I Ain't Mad At-Cha, you dig, cause I love me some sisters, always have, always will.

Can someone, will someone, preferably black and female over 35 please explain to me this recent trend that I and many of my black male compatriots have noticed lately out there in the hoods all across America. Where many single, females, professional and non-professional alike, generally over 35, usually living alone, are not so lonely these days! OK, OK. It wasn't so long ago I recall, where I only heard about and even saw examples of dog being man's best friend (you know, like Lassie, Benji and Beethoven). Now it appears the tables are turning, cause more and more sisters be coming home and riding around with these big four-legged pets lately! I can only guess at the underlying causes, but I suspect that as one "educated" sister told me (when I began questioning my imagination)—"*Well, Big Earl, think about it—with a guard dog as your companion, you don't have to worry about him cheating on you, lying to you about where he's been, or even telling anyone how much you both love each other.*" Say What!

Girlfriends, maybe dogs are becoming some women's new best friends! Especially those not-so little French poodles, and yeah those big black dogs some sisters be keeping so well fed (I know two women like this). I nodded affirmatively, when one of my homies said, "*man, us brothers had better start paying more attention to our more daring sisters, and this startling pet-trend!*" Granted, there may be a shortage of qualified (whatever that means) black men to go around, but you can bet your sweet-asses there's no shortage of four-legged dogs. As a different sister told me recently (during my doggy-girl research) yep, she owned a big, black beast. "*Well big brother Earl, I told a recent date of mine, my dog Butch didn't bite, and he didn't usually! Until my date grabbed me from behind and tried to sneak a kiss while Butch was in the room. He bit him on the ass so quick! Big Papa (Butch) was only trying to protect me... no shit! After that I never saw him again.*"

Lord have mercy-what some folks (both male and female, I'm sure) will do, when they're lonely and/or desperate for love! To all those sisters with them new canine-companions (guard-dogs guarding whatever), how about you all doing a little more work on yourselves first, before going out and spending hundreds of dollars on a vicious/jealous animal such as taking classes on building up your self-esteem, or lessons on how to have a rewarding relationship with a black member of the opposite sex. How about exercising more to lose a few of those unwanted extra-pounds, and even be willing to risk a little more against your dating fears. I truly believe this advice may work out better for you in the long run than some of you continuing to break animal-usage laws in most states! Besides, a "*two-legged dog*" has got to be better on you (OOPS! for you), than a four-legged dog! At least he can feed himself, and help pay the rent, and also (most importantly) assist in the righteous propagation of our race! Please keep in mind my beautiful and not so beautiful brothers and sisters, many a pet can get you wet (even a goldfish), but only another human-being can be a true companion! Isn't this how God intended it to be? If I ever take in a stray, she'll have only two-legs, measure in at 38-28-38, and be house broken, in good health, black and proud, and sexy as hell, period! Keeping in mind—there is no such thing as a free ride any longer! Every human action has its resultant consequences, even in-action! Brothers and sisters know this and need to act accordingly. Ever since Eve seduced Adam to take a bite off that damn sweet-smelling juicy apple, we're still trying to find real love even at our local dog pounds, damn! Lately, I've noticed on many slick

T.V. commercials, dogs beginning to talk as good as people. I hope they can keep secrets better than we do. Oh if only walls could talk, would they also bark and howl? Brothers got too much competition already. We should ban all French poodles, or at least find out what makes them so popular as pets!

LAWSUITS AND SEXUAL HARASSMENT

Oh hell yes! I just got to give a little serious advise to some of my black sisters and brothers, who can't wait, it seems for the chance or opportunity (even to initiate it) for filing a frivolous or vindictive sexual harassment lawsuit against one of their own black brother or sister associates or co-workers these days! No, I didn't say against their bosses or supervisors, government or private employers. Everybody slightly slighted these days, seems to be quick to scream, "*Show me the money! I think I've been sexually harassed!*" This can become, if it hasn't already, a very dangerous trend among black people. The reason being that any kind of personally motivated and/or ill-conceived lawsuit (or ill-timed), quite often has a way of turning out against the suit-bringer (go ask Ms. Anita Hill). Also, the process is usually always costly, especially if you lose the case, and can result in additional legal actions, like counter civil charges being taken against the initiator of the first suit.

Consider also that some recent studies appear to indicate that brothers are themselves becoming increasing motivated (probably for similar reasons—like cash) to file their own sexual harassment suits! Sooo... black brothers and sisters hoping for a large windfall from bringing a lawsuit should be extremely cautious when deciding when, and against whom, they want to sue! Especially if it's a lawsuit against another black person! Often times when this happens, it creates much media fodder (the old divide an conquer strategy) for white folks, that is generally then used against the positive hard-won (and long-worked for) self-image of black people in America. Once again, especially if both black parties to the suit are prominent members of the same company, organization or community (go ask Mr. Ben Chavis)... Truly, the long term effects, not to mention the financial loss could be devastating to you especially if a court finds no real evidence of any injuries or loss you claimed you suffered. Black people should keep in the forefront of their minds, that its the lawyers usually (both black and white), male or female that eventually makes out, or off, with the real loot! One will probably get handsomely paid (the winner), while the other, if he's lucky, will probably get laid, to ease his bruised ego. So please try and remember my "*macho-sisters and sensitive brothers*", the spoils of war don't always go to the so-called victorious and the sword of sexual harassment lawsuits cuts both ways. Try seriously talking first, ok? Ok… peace out!

SHORT STREET CONVERSATION—A SNAPSHOT

"I thought I told you that we won't stop, I thought I told you that we… hey Earl, Earl, look at that fine young sister over there—gripping that Cadillac!" I keep telling you Bro, you need to get out more often, dog! Yeah, that young sister is fine, but she's trifling and filthy! "What? Why would you say something like that rock-hard?" Well her mother is even finer than that, and she's got more class. We used to kick it back in the day, before it became popular for women to become gold-diggers, and she told me many times, her daughter was in the habit of changing her panties each and every day, but she couldn't get her to bathe but once a month! "Whaaat! No shit, dog? Well, it's her mother's fault, isn't it? I mean she must have raised her that way, right?" Shut up, fool. Didn't I just tell you her mom's got more class? I made sure of that. She bathed with me every day, I was there, you see? Now that woman over there, I mean that little girl, is 28 years old, and the little skeezer drives a new Cadillac every year! I was in her car once going to pick up her moms for a reunion she just had to have with me, and the smell of cheap perfume over all that body funk gave me one hell of a headache!

"Damn Player, maybe I'll skip bathing for a month and see if my luck will change, and maybe I can get a Caddy to grip!" If you do punk, you can no longer ride shot-gun in my Eddy-B, nigger! Plus, I'll plant a pound of bud on you, so you'll get arrested and spend the rest of your horny-ass life up in the joint! Jack-town will make you bathe each and every day, even if you don't wear no panties. "Nigger, please! Ok, ok. Rock, I was just talking, just bullshitting. If we run into little Ms. Dirty-draws, again, please let me be the first to beat her nasty-ass down, ok?" Yeah, somebody should have a long time ago. There's no excuse for anybody, male or female, running around looking good and smelling like a damn pig-hauler. Shit, soap and water is just too easy to come by!

"Yeah, true that, true that my bigger brother. With all this deadly shit out here these days who in their right mind would lay down with that squirrel?" You would! " What!?

Fuck you, Rock! Take me home, nigger." Naw, not yet, we got some gold-digging to do ourselves, bet! "Ok. I got some bud. You got some rubbers, right?" Always!

"Well, it's getting dark out and we both be wearing sunglasses. So hit it! Let's rock and roll! Unlike those Blues Brothers who wasn't brothers and didn't know shit about singing the blues! Let's do this, the ladies be waiting on big-papa! So pass me the blunt. Where's the blunt?" You need to take your ass to church, nigger. Yo, my brothers, what the hell we really talking about? Not a damn thing! "Then why are we talking at all? Now that's a serious question." Man, that brother is always serious! Drive Rock, just drive!

My brothers, dig this. My old bird always told me, Earl, if you don't have anything positive to say about someone, especially your own people, then just don't say anything at all! Do you understand, black man? "Damn, now that made me thirsty, stop at that liquor store Rock, I gotta have me a Mystic! "Make it a six-pack of Mystic, nigger, I got five on it.

"Damn that Big Earl, that nigger always trying to school somebody! Shut-up fool, he might hear you, then I got to listen to that shit all night. Especially if you keep calling him nigger!"

F.O.I. Sometimes it pays not to listen in on other's conversations, either at work, at school, or at home, or even in the back seat of a short street conversation. Next time, you could be the topic of conversation. True that! True dat!

A LADY AND HER GIRLFRIEND

Hell yeah! Men talk to one another just like the ladies do. So here's something for all so-called players (male and female). For the last time, will all you young brothers (married or single) in love with a lady, please pay attention to this! The next time one of you comes home (or to her house) and catch your wife (or girlfriend) in bed, naked, getting her groove on with another woman—- oh, damn! Do not, I repeat, do not hit the ceiling and start tearing up shit! Under no circumstances should you pitch-a-bitch (literally), or move too fast to condemn what you thought was your pussy! Reality check, my brothers, it (that good thang) was never yours, but had belonged to her (your lady/girlfriend) all the time! Keep in mind, that this is just another opportunity to make two good friends! So sit your ass down and chill (if this happens to you), and then say to them both, something like "*please ladies, don't stop, it's OK, honestly, please just allow me to watch, just act as if I'm not here*", because if you do anything other than join in, you'll lose all the way around! Especially if someone gets hurt because of a bruised ego or misplaced trust, so you felt. Think about it! Sure, love can hurt at times, but true love is forgiving, tolerant, and a healing force. So, if you ladies can't continue to love him, after discovering he's gay, just walk away, don't run away angry and vindictive and shit. Just walk away, feeling better that you now know and won't have to guess any longer about him and Tyrone. Know this, it's true of love in all cases—it's better to have experienced love and lost, than never to have loved at all! Or to choose (thereafter) to never trust or fall in love again. To do so would be masochistic. My grandfather told me a long time ago, that there was a big difference between sex (getting some) and love (giving some), and if you ever got hurt in the process, learn from it, grow from it, then keep trying until you get it right! Thanks, grand-daddy. Dig this, today, (after much of my own healing and continued growth), some of my best friends are Lesbians. Sometimes, I get to watch, but not to touch which is still cool because, watching friends do some of the crazy shit that they do is still good fun! So calm down my people, try not to be so reactionary. It's better to chill and possibly make a new friend or two than to end up on Prozak and keeping yourself company in jail, right? Right—-right!

A GREAT LITTLE PRAYER

Oh Great God of the universe
The same loving Father/Mother of all black people…
Continue to help and assist the younger ones of us,
Especially the littlest black people (the children),
Always protect them and keep them safe—FROM SOME OF US,
Some of the bigger black people.

Please God, forgive us, for we have copied and acquired so many of the bad and sad habits of white people, we now know not what we do, or why we do it, often to our own children!

Yes we, black people, inflict way too much pain and suffering on our own people, and in our own families, it is not enough to simply ask why? To save ourselves, we all (black people especially) must continue to risk a part of our lives — to protect and care for our own, because eventually, "*we all gon die*", so why not be down for the greater cause the unification and future salvation of all black people around the world and then only then, Father, should we be allowed to rest in peace and our little ones will no longer fear life in the hood– in any city, in any state, in a country that brags "*In God we Trust*!"

RELIGIONS HAVE CAPTURED MILLIONS

There are hundreds of black Catholics in this country,
Even more white Catholics,
There are hundreds of black Jehovah's Witnesses in this country,
Even more white Witnesses,
There are hundreds of thousands of born-again Christians in this country,
Even more white born-agains,
There are hundreds of black Muslims in this country
Even more kind-of-white Muslims,
There are hundreds of black so-called Jews in this country,
Even more kind-of-white Jews,
There are hundreds of thousands of black Protestants, Methodists, Mormons, and lately, a large group of Promise-Keepers coming to town soon.

With most of these religious groups claiming they all serve the exact same God. Yet their congregations utterly refuse to sit down to dinner with one another. Then secretly, behind closed doors of their respective churches, or synagogues, and temples, they preach to the flock that only <u>they</u> serve the one true God! And everyone else is simply misguided! (Probably because all of their respective robes don't match?). I often wonder why this is so.

Still I'm very confused (and I know damn well I'm not alone), why is it that most of our largest religious organizations and churches proper are still segregated by race in this country, much more so than in the east? If God is indeed a loving, just, and color-blind deity, as most groups above continuously profess or preach that He is, then why would He (your God) continue to allow this racism to exist amongst most of His followers, and continue to accept their hallelujah— praises, holy shouts, dogmatic-sexist rituals, and unholy racial segregation (not to mention the spiritual separation existing between these various groups)!

Could it be that most western religions have become nothing more than big corporate-style businesses, giant fashion and auto shows, political propaganda machines (what ever happened to the separation of church and state), or sectarian, materialistic, gown-wearing, money-getting empires—here in America? Personally I wonder what the founders and current leaders of these groups would say to God if He (God) were to hold court today in their eloquent and lavish temples and edifices! (by the way, just what the hell is a Christian-Scientist, sounds like an oxymoron to me for real doe) I bet many would whisper under their breaths, *"Oh shit! I'm not ready for this, Damn Lord, why now?"*

I can hear a lot of them now screaming at the tops of their voices, *"Oh God, oh Lord, please, it's truly not my fault! Honestly, my white pastor, black minister misled me!"* and *"Oh Father, I was always told not to question, just accept what the Church teaches—as the true will of God! and My child, our God moves in mysterious ways and cannot be fully understood,"* and on and on! Might I ask a couple of serious questions right here? First off, why-oh why is it that many of our born-again brothers and sisters can never explain to me what the hell happens to them, whenever they find (or redefine) their religion, particularly after years of raising all sorts of hell, and kicking the shit our of their brothers and sisters in the family and in the Hood. Ya'll know who you are!

Everybody black knows someone black who claims to have recently experienced a spiritual conversion, or have suddenly found salvation at the local corner church. I've lived down the street for eight years from two very large churches, who have yet to come to my aid too close two crack-houses down, on the same side of the street, where they (the Godly) park their cars! Will someone please explain to me why it always appears to me that the cost to black folks who find religion, is their blackness? These new holy-rollers immediately lose all racial pride, and even stop talking black, dressing black, walking black, and absolutely refuse to engage in any black protest or boycott of some neighborhood evil, that's affecting them as well as their brother and sister residents in the same city-block! I'll ask my more pious bothers and sisters in a heart-beat, just what is it about Christianity (for example), that causes a black person to lose all race consciousness and self-pride? All the while their white Christian counterparts continue to practice racial segregation in their homes, schools, communities, and churches within the same religious organizations and denominations!

Some will answer when asked this question, by saying that their church or religious tenets, prohibits them from looking upon the world in a worldly way! In other words don't see what is—just see what we want you to see, oh, I see! Or that their church leaders implore (preaches) them to distance themselves from issues of race (meaning I guess, racial issues are only of this world and not the next?), unsaved family and old friends, any sinner (supposedly those who need saving the most) who don't or won't believe as they do? Damn, and most black churches today seem to be filled to capacity with available and lonely black women, if any brother wants to work overtime in picking the preacher's lock on them! Second question, I guess, Why has it been for so long (here in America), so damned hard for black people to come to fully understand and know by now—in their heart of hearts what simple racial segregation means as it's practiced by their white Christian (for example) brothers and sisters, in churches and religious communities all over America!

That this type of continuous behavior on their part (white folks) is evil! And that it has always been based on their inherent fears of black people, hate of black people genes, and self-preservation politics of white power! I've said it before and I'll say it again, If your church, or religion, group, sect, spiritual cult, or whatever, has not, does not, or has never advocated or preached inter-racial peace and love, encouraged inter-faith and racial-tolerance, why on earth would black people embrace such a group?! Why in God's many names, would anyone black continue to participate in, and give their support (their time and money) to maintain such an obvious sham of real spirituality?! Of what real value would these types of groups be to black people?! If God is not a God of color-consciousness at all? Unless the God we're speaking of is indeed a white-God, then most of today's fashionable religions and Holier-than-thou bullshit works for white people, and only serves to keep black people submissive and controllable! This would explain why for many of us (skeptics) it just doesn't work, because we see beyond the lies and religious hype! Nor has it worked to save our black communities or cities, or even our souls from committing new sins and embracing all forms of evil in America these days? One day black people en-masse will come to know and accept this long standing and soul-liberating truth, "*that the religious right or (so-called) righteously-religious are indeed neither!*" "*They*" (those who use God or religion to manipulate and control black people's thinking) are neither truly religious or right!

I say, go ahead and pray over it! Pray hard and long, I know I do! Especially if you're black and still searching for God, you truly need to! Yes, I've been praying, meditating, studying for a true understanding of God and my relationship to Him and things divine and spiritual for most of my life. Oh hell yes, my soul's work paid off for me in many ways. Years ago for example—I was blessed to hear the voice of an angel which came to me and my soul in a local jail cell (honestly). This light of God suddenly surrounded me and spoke to me during one of my darkest hours. The light spoke to me with a celestial voice and said "*my special child, hear me and hear me well, even Gods on occasion fail to remember and recognize that they are indeed Gods themselves!*" The voice went on to say that "*segregation in any form, comes not from your Creator, but is indeed an evil creation of mankind, and mankind is not yet civilized in America and many parts of the world!*" It said, "*look not upon the written words of man to find your heaven or the soul's map that directs your heart and spirit homeward, instead look within yourself—it is enough, it is all that's needed, and know that God—your father—is within you.*" I can recall saying out loud back then, Amen to that brother angel or spirit or whatever you are—Amen to that!

I can hear some of my friends whispering already "*Damn it, Big Earl, why you go and rock this boat? God's gonna get you brother! He sho will! Just you wait and see!*" I can't wait to ask these friends just what God are we talking bout? The white one that owns all the land in America, or the rich one that wears the fancy crown with all the precious stones in it on those supermarket calendars, or the one with clothes on, or the one that walks around naked as a jay bird? Heaven forbid it be the one whose voice is like deep-thunder (like James Earl Jones's), whose feet are the color of fired-brass (brown and golden), and whose hair is as curly (nappy) as sheep's wool (source—The Older Bible). Now Him, I do so love to praise, and wouldn't have to fear! So tell me my so-called spiritual brothers and sisters, which God we be talking bout? I know—we know, sometimes the truth hurts! By the way, just what the hell is a black catholic, sounds like an oxymoron to me for real doe! Didn't Catholicism condone and support slavery?Yes–it did!

Yeah, unfortunately, American religions have captured millions, and sadly millions of those captured are black folks! So—will the good and meek inherit the earth! I doubt it. Damn it Mr. Religion—I demand it, "*let my people go*!"

THE BIGGEST MYTH

Is "*we must die to experience the true state of heavenly bliss*". Why is it so damned hard for most black people to reconcile the God/bible/religion given to them so long ago by white people? With the spirit of God that is felt inherently residing within their heart of hearts? Oh God, what part of who we are (the physical, mental, spiritual, aspects of our trinity) must die before we can come to know bliss(You)? Everywhere I go, it appears white folks are enjoying heaven on earth. Western religious history says the same.

Why, pray tell, is this question I'm dying to ask, so hard for us to answer? Who were my ancestors God? And why did he (or they) forsake black people in our new land (America)? Why must we have to die a physical death to experience God or our celestial home? How long must black people continue to live in a false-God-filled-land like materialistic America, with our hearts filled with suffering and pain, and persecution and loneliness from being born black? Or even worse, being proud of our blackness and natural spirituality?

No Father, no. Reassure us of our eternal oneness with Thee, and the truth that we need not die or cease to live in the here and now to experience a true God-filled relationship with you. It's true, a 10,000 year old secret has now been retranslated from ancient hieroglyphics to the way it was originally written <u>for</u> black people. The great secret says "*God is the blackness of space and time, and his offspring are those children of the dark, the ones who needed and helped to create the first light, so many eons ago, so that they might be able to see the truth, that their God is indeed within them and always have been.*" The great secret is no secret at all. <u>They just need to remember that they are themselves Gods and know it not yet!</u>

Contrary to what we (black folks) have been falsely taught to believe, God is the blackness of space, the blackness of life, the blackness of unity (love) and the blackness of our race like the blackness of Christ. When we truly know our own real history, the biggest myth becomes a lie and the real truth, the only truth that will set us all free is "*we are indeed black Gods and know it not yet*" and only time will tell! Read, Dr. Hannibal Levine Jr's new book "*the black Gods from Sirus*"—I did!

THE CELEBRATION OF KWANZA

Just another unchained black thought I'd like to share with today's Negroes, Afro-Americans, black folks! What are you all willing to bet me—Big Brother Earl Roberts, that if black people mess around and allow the celebration of Kwanza (meaning first fruits in Swahili, a beautiful black Christmas ritual) to die out through lack of participation and negligence, then it won't be too long afterward when what little culture we know of as Black-Americans will no longer exist in this country! There will be no one to blame but our ignorant selves! History has shown us over and over again—that as a people's culture goes, if it declines or grows, so will the people!

Black people must embrace and spread the joy and light of Kwanza around the known world. We must learn it, practice it's philosophy, so our people and rich black culture won't die out! Let those of us who truly understand what is at stake, lead the rest of us on this important journey of change. It is currently estimated that over 23 million people of color practice Kwanza around the world. Wow! It should be over 50 mil.

The following are the seven principles of Kwanza, as formulated by Dr. Maulana Karenga back in 1968. <u>They are the basis for reconstructing a viable black value system</u> (a needed and new appreciation of blackness) <u>for all Afro-Americans—for the collective survival of us all</u>. Read with me here:

1. **Umoja**—(oo-mo-ja)—Unity; to strive for and maintain togetherness in the black family, community, nation, race…
2. **Kujichgulia**—(koo-gee-cha-goo-lee-yah)—Self-determination; to define ourselves, name ourselves, instead of being defined and spoken for by others of a different culture.
3. **Ujimaa**—(oo-gee-mah)—Collective work and responsibility; to build and maintain our communities together, and to make our Brothers and Sisters problems our problems and seek to solve them together.

4. **Ujamaa**—(oo-jah-mah)—Cooperative economics, to build and maintain our own stores, shops, and other businesses—and to profit from them together.

5. **Nia**—(Nee-Yah)—Purpose. To make as our collective vocation, the rebuilding and continuing developing of our community in order to restore our people to their historical and traditional greatness.

6. **Kuumba**—(Koo-oom-bah)—Creativity, to always do as much as we can in any constructive way we can in order to leave our community more beautiful (clean) and beneficial (safe) than when we inherited it.

7. **Emani—**(Ee-mah-nee)—Faith, to truly believe with all our heart in our parents, our teachers, our people, our children, our black leaders, and the righteousness and ultimate victory of our collective struggle here in America.

Kwanza is celebrated for seven consecutive days, beginning on December 26th and ending the 1st of January. The lighting of seven candles, and gift-giving is also part of this beautiful black ceremony. Those of us with real pride and understanding of what it means to be black in America today, are gratefully indebted to Professor Karenga—who obviously understood that our collective black history here in America is the art of survival and a true testament to the courage and sacrifices of many, many African slaves, black slave descendants, and black Americans of yesterday and today. Thank you Dr. Karenga, and also my brother of the One Spirit, Mr. Jeffrey L. Campbell for reminding me to include this important piece in my book. Real peace and love to you both—and Happy Kwanza, my people—Happy Kwanza forever. "*What does it gainth a black man or woman to inherit the world's total wealth, if in the process he (or she) loses his cultural identity—his soul? Nothing! Not a damn thing!*" Hell, we all know by now that Christ wasn't even born on Christmas. What else have we been lied to about white America's holidays? Now we have our own—let's support Kwanza and praise Dr. Karenga!

A FUNERAL HOME VISIT

Please excuse this intrusion my God cause I know you're very busy these days, but I need to ask you a question! Have you sir, visited a funeral home in the hood lately? I have! Six beautiful black bodies were recently on display—three chapels up, and three chapels downstairs. Brother, out of the six bodies beautifully prepped for viewing, five were younger than 30 years old! Two were 24, another two were only 18 years old each. The sixth man was 45, and the only one there that had died of natural causes! Lord, one of the 18 year-olds was named Peaches. Peaches was a young mother with two kids, a four year old boy nicknamed Peanut and a three year old little girl named Nakita Nicole, fathered by two different young men. One was OK—I guess, he had signed the guest registry—"*I'll always love you Peaches*." I overheard that the other father was now in jail, preparing to spend the rest of his life there. I heard Peaches' grandmother whispering between her sad sobbing, "why did she go back to him—why did she keep pushing him to change—she knew that boy was crazy!" I silently whispered—no she didn't cause good girls are attracted to bad-boys, I don't know why. We can tell them (our young people) over and over again that the "*stove of life is real hot, and if they are not very careful—it will burn the hell out of them!*" Yet they have to touch it for themselves anyway. Lord—should I ask any of them (our young people) if they have visited a funeral home in the hood lately? Maybe they should. One way or another—maybe they will. Lord, sometimes the choice is not always theirs. Let me pray, Oh Lord, that when they do come this way, it's because of natural causes. Too many of our young black people under thirty are needlessly dying, or are in wheelchairs, or committing suicide, GOD HELP US!... PLEASE LORD!

Note, an important message begs to be shared with my young black brothers and sisters, here "PLEASE STOP YOUR VIOLENCE TOWARDS ONE ANOTHER. REPLACE YOUR SELF-HATE WITH MORE SELF-LOVE. STUDY MORE BLACK HISTORY SO YOU'LL COME TO KNOW

WHO YOUR REAL ENEMIES ARE! JUST TO NAME A FEW: DRUGS, ALCOHOL, GUNS AND KNIVES, GANG VIOLENCE, FAST MONEY AND FAST CARS, (DRINKING AND DRIVING), UNPROTECTED SEX, NO EDUCATION OR TOO LITTLE EDUCATION, RACISM IN AMERICA, NO AWARENESS OF YOUR INNER-GOD, THE CRIMINAL JUSTICE SYSTEM (READ JUST-US), A LACK OF PATIENCE, A HARD HEAD OR HEART, AND MOST IMPORTANT, NOT ENOUGH BLACK PRIDE. It is enough for now. Remember if you will, "in truth, there are no ugly black people on the face of the earth, just a few black people with some ugly behavior..believe it! I wouldn't want to be a black teen-ager in these last days of NEW ROME if someone paid me a million bucks! Walk away from the deadly dare, my young brothers and sisters, because life is short and has no spare!

May God bless and keep you all. Your brother of the spirit—Big Earl. Peace out because you too could end up in a funeral home before it's your time!

TAKE IT ALL AWAY

Take away my religious upbringing, take away my southern roots

Take away my northern street education, take away my hard won college degrees

Take away my job, take away my career, or my welfare checks, or SSI -benefits

Take away my credit cards, take away my charge cards, ATM and Lotto numbers

Take away my political affiliations, my frat., my sory, my church choir

Take away my clothes, my Tommy Hilfinger, my Perry Ellis, my Pelle-Pelle and Mark Bucanan, my Fubu, my Donna Karan (spot Hilfinger in the hood, bet his pants aren't baggy!).

Take away my dope, take away my drinks, my drugs, my over the counter scripts

Take away my club memberships, my Sam's Club, Weight-Watchers, Balleys

Take away my Nike, my Filas, my Air Jordans, my Nautica, my ab-machine

Take away my present home, my boat, my cabin, my apartment, my backyard driveway bar-b-que pit

Take away my tennis lessons, my swimming classes, my golfing and ballroom dancing

Take away my music, my CDs, TV, movie videos, my bingo and card playing

Take away my cameras, my camcorder, my Polaroid prints, my darkroom

Take away my basketball, my foot ball, my baseball, horse racing, dog fights

Take away my new car smell, my jeep, my motorcycle, and my mountain bike

Take away my running associates, my fake friends, my wack-ass neighbors and noisy cat

Take away my junkie relatives, my racist boss, my frigid wife, my wayward daughter

Take away my history, my heritage as taught by others, my media negatively showcased people

Would someone black help me to answer this nagging question, please?

"If we take away all of the above, what pray tell would be left?" Black people need to know!

A possible answer—"*THE REAL BLACK ESSENCE OF YOU—PERIOD THINK ABOUT IT!*"

SUNDAY MORNING BLESSINGS

Thank you, Jesus! Good morning Motor-City, this is your servant and the Lord's servant also, you're listening to the Right Reverend Rob Them Blind. Oh, Saints of God, have I got the message for all my listeners today! Are you tired of robbing Peter to pay Paul? Do you need a brand new car, or you need a friend to help get you out of that worrying debt? I am that friend. My Lord! You sent me to help these people, my people and that's just what Rev. Blind is gon-do! We all need that blessed healing, so you saints out there prepare to put your faith right where it belongs, in our God—cause he's an able God! Sweet Jesus, I used to be number one—now I'm the only one. Oh yes, my blessings are real, cause I feel good today.

Good God Almighty! I got today's red hot hit, for all the needy saints of God, cause God talks to me in my prayers and tells me to help and bless his faithful flocks, those saints who can here my voice right now, and those who can come down to our temple. My house is your home, Praise God! God gives me the 3-D, so I can triple dose, triple bless all believers this day, oh yes Children of the Mighty God, if you believe, you need only bring me one little pinto bean, or one grain of rice as an offering- and watch God bless the saints that do. Do you remember He said it, you need only the faith of a mustard seed, my Lord, God is Great! So pick up that phone and call me right now! All the saints who called last week and put their credit cards on the line done received their blessings big time, and many called to say: God Bless you Rev. Rob Them, I know you're a man of God, cause you gave me them digits and Lord have mercy, I got triple blessed with money from heaven!

Many asked me what can they send me, and I tell them like I tell all the saints, give the glory to our Father in heaven and send to the church whatever they feel they can spare, or send nothing at all cause I know I'm a child of the most-high and God provides for all of my needs and those needs of the church, Hallelujah! See how I give the glory to God, cause he's speaking to me right now. On Monday and Tuesday, yes Lord, you sent pennies to rain down on us, how many? Oh yes, 820—that's 8-2-0, $8.20! Three digits for three days three ways! Ok and on Wednesday and Thursday, yes Lord, even for the rest of the week, you're telling me that somewhere 4-dogs will jump 4 fences and bite some 4 people! Well Lord, Lord, Lord! I feel you, Sweet Jesus, I know the saints will come right, cause our God is a giving god, oh what a wonderful day, the Rev. Blind is giving away three and four-ways to all the callers to this station today. Ya'll know the number, so pick up that phone and call in those faith contributions to this number—area-code 313-836-0000, a change is gonna come, cause the baby is knocking at the door, Lord! Oh Lord, I see those dogs running in a straight line for 4 blocks, that's 444 and 4444, guaranteed. I'm blessing the saints on Saturday, Lord, right here in Michigan, wherever they hear the spiritual voice of the Right Rev. Rob Them Blind! No sir Lord, I'm no joke, I'm just your servant of the most high. Oh yes my brothers and sisters, I know I love money and I want you to have money, but if you can't help me, then please don't hold me back. Oh the devil is loose in Detroit, and he's busy standing in the way of these blessings to my people, Lord. But he can't stop our love, our giving, and receiving Godly natures Lord! We know god's able Detroit, I know He is able. He always see us through. Oh the saints up in Pontiac, Michigan. And those over in Flint and Saginaw, Michigan can sing His praises, cause they all shared a mighty blessing last week. God's bingo halls in Grand Rapids were paying out plenty! Those of you who needed my blessing on Friday, my one-way, one-day blessing was covered in oil to bring in the spoils! That black cat blessing oil and incense candle I told the saints to buy paid big in that cash-five game on Friday. Who said prayers don't work? Them bills are gonna go away—right now, Lord, right today! So get on that phone and call the Reverend. There's someone on the east-side and on the west-side that needs God's blessings, needing that healing, your blessings are answered by the Right Rev. Rob Them Blind. So just call, don't be afraid—God is a loving God. What's my phone number, Detroit? Ya'll call me today, I'm feeling good about these vibrations today, yes Lord, the old red man can't stop God's own. If you need to hit, call me and if you don't got no soul, or you need that special problem taken care of, just call me and say thank you Jesus. I finally got through! Damn!

Questions for my poorer brothers and sisters—in and out of the spirit? Since when did some of our black preachers and black churches get into the numbers racket, the lottery, and bingo halls? Damn, so now I guess God is sending gambling ministers (on radio and television and through the U.S. mail) to sell us his many and much needed blessings. Have we forgotten the Right Reverend Ministers Tammy Faye and Jim Baker already? I know God's people (especially black folks) can be a forgiving people, but do we have to be so gullible and naive when it comes to our modern-day spiritual- leeches and parasites?! I believe, if a saint (real saints don't gamble no matter who tells them it's Ok—in any form, bingo included) truly wants to be blessed, then he or she should stop immediately from listening to and watching T.V. or radio ministers for their blessings (financially or otherwise), and spend their much needed funds not on oils and incense, magic charms or voodoo dolls, but on their brothers and sisters in need. Those who you know are worse off than yourselves—because you can see it with your own eyes, and not through the eyes of and lies from some rich, conniving, fast-talking, pseudo-preacher who guarantees you a Sunday morning blessing! In many black neighborhoods, the devil hangs out in some churches, and on television, and on radio. So-just who do you be giving your money to? Rev. Mike can only drive one Rolls Royce at a time. He's got 11!

Good morning black America, this is your servant and the Lord's servant also. You're listening to the Right Rev. Big Earl Roberts. Oh saints of God, I do so need a loan. Please don't send me no pinto beans or rice, what I need is some cash? Please, no coins, (too noisy) no credit cards (they can be traced), just silent Green—that quiet money. If you'll give your money to someone you can't touch on T.V. or see on radio for a spiritual blessing, hell, then it might as well be me! Right? Right! I'm selling some hot spiritual blessings to black folks, cause this is a better bet than any gambling. You see—gambling is only for suckers! You dig! In church or out, without a damn doubt… praise the Lord.

This Sunday morning's broadcast has been partially sponsored by Mr. Black Mel Carr, your superstar local used car dealer. Where you can walk in with bad credit, and drive out owing him for a house—glory be!

I DREAM BLACK DREAMS

I often dream of all black women in America coming to a spontaneous and simultaneous enlightenment. A badly needed awakening that most black men need them, to help us once again to become the fathers, brothers, friends, love interests, and the great men we were meant to be (like the great men we used to be). Because, without it (black women's nourishment and support), we won't survive long enough to become what we must become in order to survive! Speaking as a father, a brother (to hundreds in several states), a friend, a love interest, and a black man, I feel the deed that we both truly need, to once again come together to feed our collective hearts and souls, to ensure a bright and safe future for our beautiful black seeds! Let us dream a black dream together.

Isn't it true, today, real integration (between the races) and equalization (between the sexes) has not worked, and probably never will truly work in our lifetimes. Still, we must remember the old lover's rallying cry "*United we stand, divided we die.*" Without each other, we don't really stand a damn chance for long-term survival! African-American couples are twice as likely to divorce than their white counterparts. It is said that divorce rates for African-American couples are the highest in the Nation, according to "our" U.S. Census Bureau. The Census figures also suggest that 45% of all African-American women and 50% of all African-American men were married back in 1980. These numbers have continued to drop since then, whereby in 1995 only 35% of our women folk and only 42% of our men are legally coupled off (married). Why is this?

So the 21st century is beginning to dawn on us black folks. Will black women come back to black men (their rightful home) where God knows they belong? I suspect that if black men are willing to do the same, we could all greet the new century as the mothers and fathers, sisters and brothers, loyal friends, faithful love interests, and united black race we've struggled so long to become. I often dream of all black men in America coming to a spontaneous and simultaneous enlightenment. An awakening that most black women need them to become what we all were meant to become—the great black people that we are! Still too many of us refuse to believe this! I dream black dreams it seems, and wonder will my people dream this dream with me? All black warriors should be willing to fight the white barbaric Vikings that still raid our communities in search of our monies and black female gold. This shit must stop! Let us dream a black united dream—so be it! Black people are black gold!

WAY TOO DARK

They forever hate us and will fear us always—they stripped a people from their homeland, when the African continent suffered its darkest days. They stole our ancestors, then a civilized people's culture and religions and hid our riches from our children—because we're way too dark. They maimed and tortured, and violently punished a people's self-pride, the very first people who inhabit Eden. They labeled them savages, then threw them into chains—stripped them, shipped them, whipped them, until their pain wouldn't subside—because they needed their labor, and because they were way too dark.

This strong and resilient people still survived even though their blood, sweat and tears, and human sacrifices stained the new soil they were forced to labor on, where they contributed more to their master's wealth, where they gave their very souls to insure his health, where they endured more than we ever could, because they were way too dark.

These peaceful and loving people continuously fought back, until one day they were free of their master's manacles and heavy chains—even free of slavery's greater atrocities like old master's rape and even worse, his name. They still continue to look upward and march for freedom's sweet escape, from a collective "*Willie Lynch Syndrome*"—because they're still way too dark.

These beautifully-hued people still search, strive, hope, want to believe that the good life, true liberty, and the pursuit of simple happiness—was also meant to be enjoyed by them. Yet thanks to Jim Crow, a false reconstruction, and native-American style reparations—they will forever be divided, powerless and economically impoverished because the survivors of Africa's stolen human gold are still way too dark.

Who can blame these blameless people, if they do wish not to remember the lynching and leg-irons of their recent past, as many now choose to overlook and turn a deaf ear to the rising shame of racial conflicts and injuries, since O.J.

Simpson won his freedom from a racist's legal system. Where their young people are still unaware that the word "nigger" is a profane and vulgar creature, created to debase and destroy their future existence because whites still fear them as way too dark.

These strong and creative children of a historically spiritual people—need to remember that their enemies will encourage them to forget, that their genes are jewels, and their internal organs, precious commodities selling today for thousands of dollars like their whole and healthy Afro-American ancestors. These intelligent and gifted first children of God must always be protected, just because they are still—and always will be, way too dark.

"Over 140 years ago, the U.S. Supreme Court's 'Dred Scott Decision of 1857' concluded that no black person, slave or free, was or could ever be a true U.S. citizen, hence, blacks had no rights which white people was bound to respect. Since that time, the Dred Scott Decision has been repudiated and occasionally vigorously denounced. Still, the highest court in our land has yet to apologize to African-Americans or reverse Dred Scott! That's still open on the record! Note: the Supreme Court justices recently hired their first black law-clerks as of 9-99, after 142 years of discrimination and racist decision-making! Damn—I agree perhaps black folks of today are still—Way to Dark! And all black lawyers and judges in the country should be ashamed of the U.S. Supreme Court's insensitivity towards black Americans!

Reprinted with permission:
Thanks, my brothers
Ron Jones & Eddie Robinson

JAIL FIGHT

I remember when I was a younger black man, I was incarcerated over a weekend, locked down for the crime of questioning white folks (the Big-Four-White Police Officers). They said I resisted arrest for something they knew I didn't do but, I had a big mouth! So they took me to jail for the weekend. While there, I was approached by a fellow black jailee. A tuff-looking ruffian type. He strode boldly across our pen, with sort of a pimp walk, looked me straight in the eyes and said, *"Hey, boy, I've been locked up for three months over a damn bag of chips and a fucking 40 oz. beer I tried to steal."* So even before he was finished talking, I hit him so quick and hard, trying my damnest to knock the shit out of him. As he fell backwards and down, I boldly strode over to where he laid and looking down on him, simply said, *"damn fool, your freedom was worth more than that! I know mine is."* Got out of jail on a Tuesday, and never went back! Yet, I'm still asking white folks serious questions, but these days just one white man at a time, cause I ain't nobody's boy..in or out of jail! Ya'll better go ask somebody—I don't play!

It's a known fact to any intelligent black American that freedom so de-valued (or undervalued) by any person of color is a direct result of the effect of successful inferiorization! Dig this, from the book The Isis Papers, the Keys to the Colors by Dr. Francis Cress Welsing, page 243 "inferiorization is essential to the ongoing process of oppression. It ensures that the oppressors need not be troubled to hold the oppressed people constantly under gun and key to keep them in the oppressed state. It keeps the oppressed from effectively challenging the oppressive power and system. In this way, the oppressor mold the oppressed to share fully in the process of their own oppression. In the final analysis - the process of inferiorization is designed specifically to prevent the maximal development of the genetic potential of the non-white oppressed. Black people must learn that no system of oppression ever maximally develops those whom the system is specifically structured to dominate (in spite of our herculean efforts to live free and equal). Such a system only permits the oppressed (black folks) to survive, so that they can continue being oppressed." Scream with me - NO JUSTICE, NO PEACE! Say it again! Dr. Welsing - may God continue to nourish your courageous soul and protect you. You are indeed the Mother Theresa of all black people today, and the Isis Papers, our new bible of survival - bet!

A BLACK COLLECTIVE GIFT TRUST (THE WHISTLE-BLOWER FUND)

Note: To all black intelligent readers of this book—Please keep in the forefront of your minds as you read this truly important piece, the simple question of asking "*why not*?" Let's think real hard about this idea! The Black Collective Gift Trust—organized and founded in (when we decide to do it!) and brought to the world by a group of prominent and wealthy blacks, who saw the need and the value of such a new black organization—particularly in America. The group's founders and board members consist of wealthy black business people, entertainers, movie and T.V. personalities, black judges and lawyers, and wealthy black sports stars (they all know who they are, and so do we).

THE MISSION STATEMENT/PURPOSE

To establish and maintain a monetary fund via biannual (large and small) contributions by members on the board of directors, trust-sponsors and members at large. To schedule and hold annual fund raising "*televised telethons*", and other promotional programs to raise money from the general American public. The motivational theme Money Talks—and Tells as Well.

Aspect #1, an annual gift-giving list of ten Friends of Black People (F.O.B.P.) nominated and selected nationally with the term "*gift*" meaning monetary gift, given to certain individuals for the specific and expressed purpose of having exposed or personally risked their life or liberty, to uncover or expose racism, large-scale discrimination, or any prosecutable act of inflicting physical or mental (provable) pain or suffering upon any black person(s) within the continental United States, including Alaska and Hawaii.

Aspect #2, the Annual Friend of Black People Award. Being the largest monetary gift to be given out. (Federal taxes would be the sole responsibility of the recipients)—This award would be known as the "*Golden Humanitarian Award*" AKA the John Brown Medal of Truth, for the courageous and unselfish action of exposing (turning in) those enemies of black people here in this country! Any person (white or black) or other nationalities, who have demonstrated (after a thorough and complete investigation) that concrete evidence exist that a person, organization, company, or governmental or private agency or public entity is guilty of practicing illegal, overt-discrimination, racism, or any destructive behavior towards black people, or promoting, publishing, broadcasting, or engaging in any activity that shall harm by intentional fraud, deceit, or political/economical cheating, stealing or injurious deeds to the health and welfare of the general black public citizens of all of these United States! Anyone who can be brought into a court of law, local, state and federal courts). to be used, to redress (and prevented from continuing to commit) a grievous wrong against black people. All selected friends of black people who have assisted or informed the governing committee (Board) shall be honorably and handsomely rewarded for their exposure or evidence (after the arrest and/or civil/criminal convictions) of the enemies or prosecutors of black peoples rights and lives. They shall have their names and deeds inscribed—(ceremoniously) in the Book of Justice and Honor—For the Friends of Black People.

Aspect #3—The annual list of ten Friends of B.P. Shall receive at least $100,000.00 from the Trust (in the form of a monetary gift) because money talks and bullshit walks, and it also motivates more watchers for the cause of protecting black folks interests and lives. The annual recipient of the Golden Humanitarian Medal of Truth—shall receive a certified check from the fund, in the amount of $250,000.00. Note: After five years of operating and soliciting contributions from the black and white general public, and trust sponsored fund-raising, the annual gifts (each categories) shall be raised by $25,000.00 per award and to continue on every five years thereafter to further motivate people of good conscious to come forward.

Aspect #4, the above is only a rough draft, of an idea whose time has come and which has been needed in America for a very long time. This organization, the (United?) Black Collective Gift Trust would be a true boon to honest and hardworking black people (i.e., black jellybeans of Texaco) all across America. To aid and assist all black Americans in their time of need, in their search for justice and equality, in their pursuit of fairness and protection under the constitutional laws of this land. It is an undisputed fact that black people are burdened unnecessarily, unjustly, and often illegally due to their shared blackness here in America. To insure that our kids and young people receive their just rewards and proper recognition in the future, we need to continue the struggle for their right to exist and live at peace in this so-called great melting pot of various nationalities -without having to continue to look up (and struggle) from it's bottom and beg for crumbs off of America's table of plenty! Question to my people, those that are rich and those not so rich, Why not? We need a new black vanguard in America, a true and powerful national black sentinel. We need the United Black Gift Collective Trust Fund!

We need to start today—we need to honor all our true friends and courageous allies (and there have been many who have given their lives for black freedom). Because history has shown us (and sadly continues to show us) we cannot win the fight of simple equality and justice for black people in America alone! Someone, anyone, must get on the phone, write those letters , spread the word... one to one, and to the Black masses everywhere! Ask all of the 100 or so Black multi-millionaires in this country, (Oprah, Bill Cosby, Michael Jordan, Eddie Murphy, John H. Johnson, Dave Bing, Mel Farr, Don Barden, Berry Gordy and many, many others), which one of them will be the first to donate $250,000.00 to ignite this great and noble cause?

Ask each of them who will be the first to be honored as a founding black father or mother, to go down in history as a truly concerned and caring black leader who was courageous enough to see the need to build a permanent, active, black-sentinel unlike any human-rights organization the world has ever seen? We must ask each of them (their names and addresses can be found at the main libraries in every major city, hint—go and look them up under America's Wealthiest Blacks) if they would be interested in investing in the creation and building of a National Black Watch-Dog Trust Fund similar to the ones that white-folks and Jewish people have? Would they be willing to lend their good names and monies to support and implement this noble, well deserved tribute to 50,000,000 of their own peaceful and patient black brother and sister Americans—through this "*United Black Collective Gift Trust*" idea. It could quickly become a powerful and glorious reality if we collectively believe it, yes we can achieve it.

If black people, as a courageous and united people constantly, vigilantly, continue the struggle for self-sufficiency and empowerment, through the daily efforts of the black wealthy and the not so wealthy, to strengthen and protect the human and civil rights of all Afro-Americans. We can do this, and if we do this, there will be nothing that can hold us down! No force, be it the U.S. government, white-racists, of a national, public, or private source, will succeed in turning millions of black Americans into second-class, impoverished, powerless citizens! The next century is dawning and time will tell, and so will the enemies of black people, if they know that money is involved in the process! I say let us try it. Hell, it couldn't hurt (at least we'd get to know which black millionaires are still black and proud of it), and this just might be the counter-weight to America's deep-seated racism that might ultimately lift-up our black race. While at the same time, expose more of those individuals, companies, organizations, and businesses that continue systematically, and intentionally set out to hurt black people due to the color of our skin. To aggravate the negative effects many of us still suffer from, due to the scarring of black American's conscious because of slavery's evils here in America. So, black Americans, everywhere this book shows up should pass the word, talk it up, and always remember—united all of us will stand (survive), divided—we all will fall (cease to exist)! To my beautiful black people, please believe it! We know it could happen! Can we do this thing? Yes, we must do this thing! Right ? Right! Big Brother Earl says, I'll be honored to be the first black man to donate $500.00 to this truly worthy and badly needed fund. Bet. Talk it up! Talk it up! "*A people without a vision—is a people who shall perish*" (Proverbs).

THE VALUE OF SCHOOL

Of course it bears repeating, our children need the best education they can get! We should constantly remind them that, not too long ago, it was illegal and dangerous for black people to attend a school of any kind! An education is a strong weapon against slavery of the mind and a must have to ensure one's continued freedom in a country that charges a king's ransom for it. If our young Brothers and Sisters refuse to go to school and get a good education, then they won't have a future! Think about this real hard! We (those of us with knowledge) must find a way to make them listen! It's always easy to point fingers, so let's point them into a mirror! The value of school is that it's still free (for the most part) and truly invaluable! Oh yes, for those parents who can afford to send their kids to private schools or academies—you ought to sneak up on them once in a while and catch some of those little spoiled and selfish brats misbehaving worse than some of their public school counterparts! If you discover I was right—no need to thank me, just give your neighbors kids a helping hand (or hug) when they need you to. let's teach our young how to fish (learn) so they can feed themselves for life! As opposed to many so-called black middle class parents giving them a fish to eat for one day or night. Each one (black adults) should reach out to one (doesn't have to be your own) to teach one—how to fish! We can do this! We must because no other race will do it for us.! Bet! Each and every black child must be taught true Black History early on, and continuously until college. An education without one's true history being included is not true knowledge. Without an awareness of our past, there are no roots to our future. They (the children and all black adults) must know from where they came in order to know where they are going. Believe it! Around the turn of this century (1900s), many states under their "separate but equal policies", through their departments of education, allocated on average $5.00 to educate a black child compared to approximately $50.00 for a white child, then came integration 55 years later and things got worse! In 1993, I recall the numbers had only slightly improved. Today, education of black youths is like a state lottery in support of education—blacks seldom win the big one!

THE NEW BASKETBALL YOUTH CONSPIRACY

Yes, because of successful brothers like Michael Jordon, Grant Hill, Dennis Rodman and Shaq, now throw in corporate greed, enormous profits from a river of fancy gym shoes flowing into urban black America, and our black shoe-fetish dollars flowing out of our cities—back into the coffers of white blood thirsty capitalist and what do you have? We have a situation that's ripe for disaster for black Americans of all ages. Check this out!

Several athletic shoe manufactures are silently and smoothly raiding black urban grade schools (damn)! To find and groom from an early age our talented and tall black youth to rob them (by buying them young) of their futures, and to profit off of them big time when they reach the tender age of consent- all across America these days.

Yeah—we can throw in the black parents of these highly sort after six and seventh graders, who are just as responsible for this recent and continued corruption of their own sons and daughters (especially young black males), because they also have never been offered so much, so soon, with future "*promises*" of millions of dollars to some, if their children become good enough—coming out of high school, turning pro, and playing basketball, baseball, or football (like Kobe Bryant).

They are telling our kids, that through future peer and public recognition from playing "*B-Ball*", they will become walking billboards for the shoe companies and make all kinds of crazy paper (millions), while having their choice of succulent groupies (girlfriends, etc), and other tempting and unbelievable half-truths to keep them in training! Keeping them and their parents from ever considering other options for these young brothers and sisters. These gym-shoe makers don't tell them that they are actually gambling only a little money now (on the backs and feet of our golden youth), so that they in turn will be in position to sell hundreds of millions of shoes, shorts, socks, jock, sweatsuits, and other athletic accessories—to make an unimaginable amount of money off of our children who can't play ball or read a contract!

Believe it!... In the news lately, companies like NIKE and ADIDAS and several others (the majority of which are still white owned and operated), are indeed spending millions of dollars on "youth summer camps", equipment, and gym shoes (supposedly free)—for those schools and kids who are the best potential future (marketable) stars of professional sports! They swear it's not an investment in black-bodies, yet they know if they can get their hands on a future Michael J., then their own kids—the kids of the company owners and shareholders, will never have to work for a living for the next five generations to come! Recently you'll recall a black high school graduate- (?) was offered 123 million dollars to play professional ball! Presently, several junior high school kids are being "*courted*" by the giant shoe companies. These young black charges were treated to trips to (of all places) Las Vegas, and other questionable locals, given gifts and luxury items that most adults continue to dream of and have problems with—even when they can afford to purchase these for themselves! We need to pay closer attention to what's really going on!

Truly in today's highly competitive "*informational*" society—our talented urban black youth need to be constantly warned and told, that they have a better chance and better odds, at becoming doctors and lawyers- than superstar athletes! Somebody should ask Dr. Dennis Kimbrow- (author of "Think and Grow Rich- a Black Choice 95") why this is so imperative today! He'll tell you that our children are being truly misled and deceived! By big sports promoters and gym shoe companies! Yet due to this quiet conspiracy by the shoe makers and their cohorts, the wolves of the big Madison Ave. Ad-Agencies. Our young (as young as 10 years old and their unaware Parents) are being set up (prepped) for the new slave sports markets of the future! The search has already heated up and has been ongoing for over 10 years now!... .The race is on pay attention! THIS IS SOME SERIOUS SHIT!

Which athletic shoe maker will be the first to find the new (black-faced) superstar, who will be brought and sold (controlled) by the NIKE or FILA of tomorrow, before he reaches the ninth grade in school! To be used to help them continue to legally rob and misguide millions of our young black boys and girls all over America! I can't help but wonder, which black national organization (The Urban League—the NAACP, etc)—or black courageous member of congress, will be the first to sound the alarm about this serious, dangerous, intentional, distraction (nationally) of "*our precious kids*" away from a quality twelfth grade education at least, towards a false hope and a one-in-hundred-thousand chance of appearing on national TV, dribbling or throwing a ball, in his (or her) underwear, talking about jumping higher because of the re-act juice in his sneakers, which may earn him big status in the hood out on the black top, but will surely cost him months of allowance at the least, or maybe his future dreams of a quality—college degree or career education at the most!

Please, my people, somebody black, courageous, and attentive, (or some truly loving black parent) had better start asking some hard questions real soon! The year 2001 may be too late for us (black folks) to intercede in the continued legal (yet, decisive and debilitating) rape and pillage of our future black leaders, our defenseless children. Isn't it truly sad that still in this day and age, many black people can't (or refuse to) recognize and see the forest (blood money) due to the trees (gym shoe companies) that set money traps for our kids and pretend they're doing black people a favor! Personally, I hope I never see a black thirteen year old NBA walking billboard, or another black teenager proudly walking around sporting the word FILA, cut into the back of his head, damn!

SAVING FOR TOMORROW

Save, save, save, please my people!
Learn to save some of your money—part of your income! You'll never know when funds may be needed. Savings can turn your life around for the better—for your good. he who controls the gold—makes all the rules!

Save, save, please!
Set aside some of your earnings early on—it doesn't matter the amount, yet, the more the better. Savings can grow exponentially because of interest earned. It costs money to borrow money. don't borrow it—save it!

Save, save, save, please!
Black folks must learn all over again how to save. Our financial resources are usually a lot less than other races. Savings give us clout, credit-power, peace of mind, etc. Brothers got to bring more to the table than others!

Save, save, please!
Your future will improve in direct proportion to the monies you have saved, or begin to day to save. Opportunity beckons all too often, when funds are all too non-existent or too low. Learn to invest in interest earned!

Save, save, save, please my people!
Start to save something, any amount, because it's true—a single penny saved is two pennies earned. Saving money is almost unheard of in the Black community. Realize—savings creates wealth and provides monetary emergency assistance when life depends on it. Negroes had better start saving fast and big—white folks are now screaming, "*Negros should stop asking us to save them—let them save themselves.*" I don't have a problem with this, our history shows we can! Bet.

How sad (but so true), dig—yes we Black people, know all too well how to spend our money/income—because America has taught us well how to spend! So what the hell! What could it hurt? If we re-learn how to save some of our hard earned money (green-backs, crazy-cash, stupid-loot, big-cheese, paper-knots, etc.) We must try and remember—if we don't begin to save for our futures, then surely if it comes, when it comes, we'll be praying for the return of (white-peoples) welfare or jobs on a cotton plantation, that pays only .25 cents an hour! Wait, some blacks love to sing (even if we don't save worth a damn)—OK, try this tune, sing—"*we can do it, we can do it—if we put our minds to it!*" Again—"*I can do it, I can do it—if I put my mind to it!*" "*In 1863 black Americans owned and controlled approximately one-half of one percent of the nation's wealth. By 1993, blacks own and control one and one-half percent of our nation's wealth. What a damn shameful fact*!"

Let us teach our children this tune while they watch us at the local black-bank or black savings and loan, opening a new savings account A.S.A.P.! Saving for our tomorrow's should become the new Negro National passion—period!

CELEBRATE BLACK HISTORY MONTH
A MINI-EPIC—I KNOW A PEOPLE

I know a people—whose roots are with the sun
Their heritage rich with a civilized history as old as mankind itself.
Even unto today, these are a people with a natural patience.

I know a people—who once respected the earth, and the sky. Who sought permission from their ancestors to feast with their animal neighbors off the land and out of abundant rivers.

I know a people—who once had before their alters, prayed to many Gods, Gods who supported and blessed them. Long before they became lost in a new world, and then came to know only one God.

I know a people—whose golden bronze hues gave the first rainbow to the world, and whose skin complimented the rays of light from above. A beautiful spiritual people whose eyes reflected a celestial wisdom.

I know a people—whose past accomplishments and greatness, still astounds the world today, with their intricate temple designs and complex pyramid structures. Whose many designs and art are collected the world over.

I know a people—whose forefathers bravely and boldly conquered the known world around them—like the pharaoh kings of Egypt, and Hannibal the Great, who united a thousand tribes—like Shaka Zulu, blackmen who bravely sailed the great oceans and seas, long before Columbus was even born.

I know a people—with a real life story to tell their children,. A story that leads from their past collective greatness unto their present insignificance. A result of horrific enslavement and it's trials and evil tribulations, in a foreign country in the west.

I know a people—whose recent history is littered with enormous wisdom teachers, blood sacrifices, stolen creations, like the cotton gin, the shoe basting machine, the gas mask, fountain pen, brown paper bag, the traffic light, soul food, peanut butter, the hot comb, blood plasma, and a thousand other indispensable things—laid claim to by the Tom Edisons and Ben Franklins of the world.

I know a people—who was taught and forced to believe whatever they were told to believe. Until one day these people, who prayed the hardest and who played the hardest finally came to realize that they were wrong for believing all they were told and led to believe, and today know not what to believe.

I know a people—who have given a great many powerful wise men and women to the world—in every era and epoch of their existence, since their first father received the name of Adam. Who gave to them a long lineage of great kings and queens, legendary warriors, sages and saints, artists, poets and statesmen, scientists, teachers, writers, actors, athletes, musicians, inventors, builders, politicians, religious leaders, peace makers, and a very visible genetic marker that refuses to be destroyed—that of color.

I know a people—who today call out to one another, side by side with society, hey black trash, what's up niggers, them non-skilled, limited education, welfare grubbing, leaching black thugs, marauding gangster wanna-bes, lazy ass coons, punk militant troublemakers, uppity second class, typical bastard blacks… where the foul word nigger is tossed around like a popular last name "*Yo, my nigger, you still my nigger, if you don't get no bigger*", and "*nigger please.*"

I know a people—who will not accept their true destiny, the truth that contains their ultimate salvation and survival, the sacred key to their future existence, which is learning

once again how to love and trust each other. To truly love themselves as a great people—and continue the fight for their God-given right to unite as one, before they can unite with a New World Order...
I know a people—where 65-75% of them still suffer from deep-rooted psychological and inherited emotional scarring from their direct descendants who were exposed to years of the Willie Lynch Syndrome. Where the psychological and physiological deadly seeds of 500 years of slavery's savage heritage, is still bearing bruised and ugly, divided fruit, as it was so intended long ago.

I know a people—whose children are still being educated by others, in schools and universities far from their neighborhood homes, and the parents wonder why their children grow into adults who actually despise themselves and their own people, then see them struggle to become anything but what they are (a great and intelligent people of color)—what God intended them to be. Where they will continue to fail themselves until they come to know self-acceptance, which starts with self love.

I know a people—who collectively spend a combined income of over 300 billion dollars a year, most of it spent in communities not their own, and where many of them are still not allowed to live. A people who saves less than 5% of this—a people who have yet to learn why other people (foreigners and recent immigrants) do just the opposite within the same country (this country) and thrive and grow rich and very powerful over time...

I know a people—a truly God-fearing people, who honestly believe like the intelligent Jews during World War 2 did, that it couldn't or wouldn't happen to them—not today, not in this great country of freedoms protected. The same country that had given them 350 years of genocidal slavery, syphilis experiments, barbed-wire project homes, 5-6 deadly and costly (in black lives) ground wars, a debilitating welfare system that kept them passive, dependent, and controllable...

I know a people—who still believe that our own western-style government would never declare martial-law over them, and force them once again into real concentration camps and bigger prisons and jails within the USA. because of its deeply rooted fear of them and their genes, and because technology and robotics has reduced labor-intensive industries to a minimum, and where black second-class citizens will have to wonder the land in search of work, food and jobs.

I know a people—who for hundreds of years, could not sleep a sound night's sleep, a restful rest, because they secretly feared their white ex-slave masters, or government, or their own National Guard, or the CIA, or FBI, may one day poison their water or food supplies, or conspire to flood their isolated and segregated neighborhoods (and rural communities) with addicting crack cocaine and automatic weapons to destroy themselves with...

I know a people—whose women-folk have been taught to believe, that beauty is Euro-centric, and programmed to accept European standards of fashion, style and cosmetic habits, and values. Who were brain-washed to believe that their men-folk were all liars, cheats, dangerous, sexual maniacs, violent and irresponsible dogs, thieving drug users, poor fathers—and while they were told to wait before exhaling, the most obvious deceit of all—that there (sadly and unfortunately) were not enough eligible black men to go around, so black women were justified to go outside of their own race to find a true provider and protector, even to marry the white sons of the eternal enemy.

I know a people—who were not too long ago proud to be black (as recently as the late 60's) who used to stand-up, sit-in, protest, boycott, march, speak up and out, while saying it loud We're black and proud! Until one final injustice befell them and all of their young had died off. Because their great western civilization to them had lied... freedom, equality, the much revered American Dream, was reserved for all other Americans, but not the black ones. It seems equal rights and affirmative-action was a mistake—declared one of their own black conservative leaders, Clown Thomas…

I know a people—that will no longer exist in the not too distant future, and their very presence will be wiped away from the pages of American and world history. All because their greatest King, failed to mention in his famous speech, "I Have a Dream", that each one (black/colored) must teach one, to never forsake their roots, the dynamic roots of their own people. In order to survive the continual black-holocaust, they must learn all over again, how to love and trust their own kind. Then no future historian will have to say—I once knew a people.

I know a people who have long been known as a strong and resilient people. The majority of which have been hardworking charitable, peaceful, non-violent, church-going, and God-fearing Christians who have nursed, fed, clothed and rescued off ghetto streets, their homeless children and adults, those who worked for and fought wars for the rights of other people here in America—for well over 350 years. Whose serious contributions and accomplishments in making this country great and a world leader today, still goes unappreciated and largely unacknowledged.

Even unto today, these beautiful, yet misguided and divided, self-loathing people curse and criticize a great living black man—living amongst them. A spiritual man who tries to teach them the truth and ancient wisdom. A honorable and enormously intelligent black man, produced by an African King's seed, and American's continued evils against her own black warriors, since King Solomon, or Mohammed the Great, or Moses, or Hannibal walked on Earth. This great light and flame, and protector of black America's consciousness. I'm speaking of the most honorable Nation of Islam Leader—Minister Louis Farrakan. A black man who initiated and led 2,000,000 black men to march and atone… He who prayed with 2,000,000 for reconciliation and forgiveness. Let at least 10,000,000 of us (black folks with understanding) pray we never lose this great black man, this home-grown (African-American) by-product from the roots of 1619! If we lose him, black America will have lost yet another great black peace keeper and a courageous black man of God.

EPILOGUE TO I KNOW A PEOPLE—
A COLLABORATION

I know a people—who from black southern roots, created two gifted northern African American brothers. One 45 years of age, the other 34, both are policemen in the great state of Michigan, in a great cosmopolitan city, the new north star—Detroit. They became close friends, who later became one on a spiritual level. Who both prayed for Rodney King and Malice Green, and who prayed for all the righteous brothers who attended the great march on Washington on October 16, 1995. Two brothers unrelated except by job and race, who continued on their respective warriors' paths (in uniform and out) to fight injustices, racial discrimination, demeaning and disrespectful attitudes towards their black brothers and sisters, and who wrote a mini-epic entitled, "*I Know A People*" and dedicated it to Black History Month, and to all black, mighty warriors past, present, and to those that will come after them. May we continue to hear form these two poetic and righteous brothers, whose united voices continue to sing the praises to their own Mrs. Rosa Parks and the former great Mayor of Detroit, Coleman A. Young. Ask them when you see them serving the public and risking their lives for their people and their city, why we should continue to build up and celebrate Black History Month all across the country. These two fearless policemen will surely respond—If you are a true black American in today's world, it is the right thing to do!

To all black law enforcement people—still black and proud—thank you! Working together, we can stop the violence against our own and reverse the negative destructive effects of self-genocide. More peace, love and empowerment can come to the black community for a beautiful people, when we stand strong and stand together again! Right on Officers Ron C. Jones and Eddie Robinson—"WCS Dept. "*Right On Blackmen*!"

THE NEW NORTH STAR—DETROIT

All our praises due to the new north star—Detroit. Long a destination of run-away slaves and freed southern blackmen seeking true freedom and peace of mind and spirit. Dee-troit, where a white man was-gon-pay a black man and his family a full $5.00 dollars a day to work in an automobile plant and keep his yard and home clean in 1950. All praises due (just 70 years later) to his most honorable (black-ass) Coleman Young. A black man's black man! A civil-rights freedom fighter, a courageous Tuskegee Airman (a Democrat), a big-city mayor, and extraordinary black leader! When President Jimmy Carter was in the White House, so was Detroit. Old Coleman would come home with millions to rebuild Detroit after her riots (which really was just an oppressed and poor black people's shopping spree), and give his people many new opportunities to become educated and wealthy. ... Yes, old Coleman lived it as he said it, he was never afraid to walk the talk!

On Liberation for All—"*No white person can be hurt by a positive struggle for black rights. What is good for black folks, who are at the lowest level of the economic and social structure in this day is good for white folks. By the same token, that which injures blacks-injures all folks. That's a hard lesson. Sometimes those who preach it die by racist acts. Others will follow to tell the story. It's the only route I know to freedom.*"

On Racism—"*Racism is something like high-blood pressure. The person who has it doesn't know he has it until he drops over with a goddamned stroke. There are no symptoms of racism. The victim of racism is in a much better position to tell you whether or not you're a racist than you are. And on the subject of white power—white people find it hard, extremely hard to live in an environment they don't control.*"

His Honor speaks for Big Earl as well when he comments on looking out for No.1: "I never looked upon myself as a do-gooder. What I've done is in my own self-interest. It serves to validate my own personal sense of worth and dignity as a

Black person, as a poor person, a person of working class origin." Yes, we'll miss you Sir, we Northern Star blacks shall never forget Coleman Alexander Young (May 24, 1918—November 29, 1997), a great contemporary black man—one whom all black folks can be truly proud of … God bless C.Y. Bet! and now—

All praises due the many blacks (actually the few who bravely represented the many, who could not—or chose not to represent themselves), who to this day, remain pro-active and truly black inside the boundaries of the big "*D*"! It has never been an easy matter for black leaders to lead black people, but these brothers and sisters, and our own Mrs. Civil-Rights Shining Star, Ms. Rosa Parks—are continuing the struggle, over here in this black-ass rich -town. A place where brothers and sisters be sitting on an old-gold-mine (some call it salt) and collectively bank more cheese (money and credits due) than they care to disclose! What's up old black-faced Michigan's Motown! Inside a white, Militia-stronghold state. I say never die, to my brothers on the front lines—with eyes that really see. To brother Lawrence X, my friends Ken, Vincent, Sylvester, Big John, and my favorite Kente cloth wearing attorneys, P. Curtis and J. Edison. Continue to show black men the right way! To Brother Kenyatta (who policed the hoods with me before it was popular), and that right Rev. Anthony (a truly unbought civil-rights leader), a church minister and President of Detroit's NAACP. You brothers better continue to watch your backs, because (unfortunately) the Willie Lynch Syndrome is alive and well in Dee-troit (as it is within many northern cities). I am one of many who are extremely proud of you all, for the inspirational example of what it truly means to be intelligent and fearless contemporary black men, thanks. Let us hope as we pray that our new mayor, his honor the "*bridge-builder*" won't give away our new Northern Star, the city-proper, new casinos (which will eat black folks alive) new ball parks and all! We've already lost our grand Belle Isle to the suburbanites and auto-racing, where tickets are so high my son and I have to scale a tall fence just to see and stand next to white folks!

Some say that white folks are trying to steal back control of Detroit's water and sewage complex. Detroit will be sorry if they succeed. King Archer could still be offered a cup of hot coffee and a job up there on Capitol Hill, by his good friend Buffalo-Bill! So, Motor City, how many of your current residents know that you were once a great way-station—a gateway to freedom on the Underground Railroad? Which led many runaway slaves to the freedom and protection that Canada offered people of color, that they could not find in America. So, where to from here, my growing, beautiful, black Northern Star? The rest of black-ass America will be watching you. Tell me Big "*D*", are you black middle-class brothers and sisters, big enough to take care of your less fortunate brothers and sisters that are still homeless and hungry and living on your city streets? Will you gangster-ass folks in the hood, wake up and realize the only ones you hurt with your physical assaults and home invasions, are your own people, family, and friends! So, check that shit in, turn down your collars my criminal friends, cause your Governor—Mr. E. has got a new prison-plan to lock you fools in! Stay black and keep your pride alive so the city-proper can prosper and all ya'll can shine like the intelligent and valuable African pearls and diamonds (males and females) you truly are! Exile your criminal activities north of Eight Mile Road… I dare you… no. I double dare you! White folks don't have the patience that blacks do! They don't tolerate crime unless it wears a white collar!

Be aware my brothers, that Mr. E. has proposed five new prisons, that the citizens of Michigan and Detroit must pay for to ensure adequate bed-space for your black-asses in the years to come. While living in Detroit for many years, I've had the opportunity to visit the three jails we already have. I've met many who work there also. To them, thanks for the tour of one of America's newest dog pounds! There is nothing like cold hard steel (bars of a cage), and the sound of slamming steel and glass doors to awaken the awareness of helplessness in some of our more misguided and violence-prone brothers and sisters. I am extremely uncomfortable with how easy it seems, for so many of our young black persons to accept the loss of their own individual freedom! I over-heard a white-turnkey yell at an inmate, "*if you really want some respect, my man, then keep your black-ass out of jail!*" Again, Jessie Jackson said it first, jail is no place to be somebody—no shit! How true it is! Black-ass Detroiters had better prepare to fight a strong fight- for what they and Coleman have worked so hard to build when the gambling starts in your new North Star! Yes you brothers and sisters inside the law and who work inside Detroit's big three jails- were absolutely correct, jail is no place to pretend to be somebody! Wake up niggers! Gambling equals freedom lost, and problems up the ass-big time! So stop doing it!

To the non-gangster and religious elements of Dee-troit, shine on you black diamonds—shine on. Oh-by-the-way, my Detroit brothers and sister, need I remind many of you with those fancy job titles and advanced college degrees—that the struggle for true freedom and equality is not over by no means even in Detroit. Since a black Detroit man must serve a life sentence for a murder-2 conviction, but two white racist Detroit police officers can go free after murdering an unarmed black man, after only serving four years in prison and all you educated and living-large black folks can't do a damn thing about it, or could you? Here's a better question—will you try to find out why not? Ok., All praises are still due to the new North Star—Detroit. Long a destination of runaway slaves and freed southern black men, seeking true freedom and peace of mind and spirit. Personally, I hope one day we'll all find it. Will blacks in Detroit show us the way? We'll soon see, because blacks all over America will be watching and so will Big Brother Earl and his little brothers 3-5-7-Bet!

TO ALL BLACK SELL-OUTS

In case any of you sold-out niggers (upper class, middle class—whatever) want to know what gives me the right to speak out on any issue regarding black people I answer by saying God gave me the right—to be born a free black man, who courageously speaks out on issues affecting my race and blackness, (because I choose no longer to turn the other cheek) including answering confused and nocuous niggers who continue to ask intentionally divisive and dumb-assed questions like the one above... period! So don't any lost brothers or sisters who refuse to study black history for whatever lame-ass excuse try and contact me at my home, my phone is tapped by the real devil (the illuminate of the west) and my walkway is lined with explosive watermelons! (Sell-outs know they're dying for a cool piece!) So house niggers, beware—black is a force to be reckoned with, black is a force to be seen! Black is still beautiful, know what I mean!

P.S. Yes—I stay strapped down! I don't go looking for trouble, but I won't be pushed around! Bet! Hell yeah!, I'm in this only to win this, for a thousand years to come, until our mutual struggle is over, or until white racism is undone!

Right on Big Earl—Right on!

LAST SEVEN PAGES—UNCHAINED

☼Attention all you black Sories and Frats—Ya'll gotta start giving more back! All that new found knowledge and skills, kinda like a new world experience, right? … . Well black guys and girls, you just gotta take it to the streets (black neighborhoods) because your little black brothers and sisters are waiting to look up to you all for some of that high-priced education and some cheap eats! Go feed their little stomachs and their minds—urban Big Brothers and Big Sisters programs need you bad! Question: is a black "*Greek*", an Oxymoron? Africans would not approve—ask any Zulu! ✸

☼To all those unenlightened black mother-suckers, always professing to be so damn poor! Listen-up one more time! All of us live in an abundant universe—and there is always enough to go around, so stop professing lack and limitations and watch your riches grow. Oh—yeah, and most important, keep your dumb-asses out of those Rent-To-Own stores, where a TV and VCR—combo will cost you five times to rent what the same exact shit sells for at Sears or Montgomery Wards. Be smart—bring back the Lay-Away-Plan! ✸

☼I just can't get over a "*dumb-nigger*" (a seriously confused black person—male or female, young or old, rich or poor, with no self-respect)—proudly running around in a Marilyn Manson sweatshirt—damn! If my glock ever needs target practice, I know my homies (look-outs) will keep track of this nigger for me—cool? Rack-rack a fresh clip, can't wait till I see him again! ✸

☼Yoh!—All you so-called middle-class negroes, I've tried to warn you—one day ya'll gonna regret spending your dollars out in the burbs! You must give back—you must buy black! You owe more then you know to past black entrepreneurs. More my sisters and brothers then to your own fathers and mothers! Remember, the straightening comb was invented by a black woman! Look it up fools under financial genocide! ✸

UNCHAINED THOUGHS CONTINUED

☼True, so true—we become what we think about all day long, my people make some time to think black, please! There is no shame for our people in this game. Black is back!✸

☼The Detroit News—Friday, October 17, 1997 / 5A Briefly, the Nation/World. Tulsa, OK—Title: Supremacist Jailed In Terrorist Bomb Plot.—A white Supremacist was sentenced to three years (only three years—Damn!) in prison Thursday for a plot to bomb 15 cities. James Viefhaus, Jr. (28)—stood mute before U.S. District Court Judge Michael Burrange, and tearfully apologized for his taped threats last year ('95) condemning blacks, homosexuals, Jews, and black people still wonder where our missing children go... ✸

☼The Detroit News—same day, same page, briefly, the Nation/World. Atlanta—More Minorities Receive Vaccines—what a title!—Damn! A record number of children of racial and ethnic minorities have received the recommended vaccinations against common ailments, federal health officials of the Center for Disease Control and Prevention said—(Thursday, October 16, 1997). They said more than 90% of Black, Hispanic, Native-American, and Asian Pacific Islander children had been vaccinated against Diphtheria, Tetanus, and Pertussis. Question: So what of the European Americans (WASP) children? Why no mention of them by the Feds? Kinda makes me wonder! You too? Maybe you should! Our future lies within our offspring.✸

☼I got some brotherly shouts to send out to those true black Wayne Country Sheriff's deputies—especially that Bad-Ass J.J., and P.T., and a few others like Berry, Vaughn, John and Ron who studied black history in America and still carry a badge. Hey Vaughn—whatever happened to that smooth-ass trusty we called Ken-Tone? Shouts out of pride and thanks to all black police officers around the country—who go on duty still black and proud. Our race will not survive without you-all! Please don't change. ✸

MORE UNCHAINED THOUGHTS

☼One more serious shout out (or for me a scream). My people—know this, within today's information rich society—there is absolutely "*no excuse for stupidity*!" It appears amongst many people, (not just our own) many nationalities that mother-wit (common sense) is in limited supply these days. People can do and say some stupid shit sometimes! Like some of your best friends are white racists—damn! Remember Garnett Johnson? ✸

☼No matter how many times we (black folks) here these words—forever is not too long. So say them often, say them loud! Self-love equals self-respect, and together they equal dignity! Way too many blacks have forgotten or never have understood why the Civil Rights struggle and riots were necessary in this country just 38 years ago. ✸

☼"We need to keep reminding our young people"—"learn nothing in this life, and the next life you live will be the same" says Chief Paulinho (Pie-A-Con) of the Kayapo Tribe of South American Indians. He also said "I *have observed for years now—even went to work for the white man to get to know his nature and intent towards our land. I have come to know in my heart that the white man was the inventor of massive destruction. My culture and the rain forest don't stand a chance. To us (the native peoples of the Amazon Rain Forest) the earth is our life. The lumber from the trees, and the gold in the earth, is all the white man cares about!*" From World News, Chief Paulinho—May, 1997. You tell them chief! Many wouldn't believe me! ✸

☼Lift every voice and sing—this rap song. Nobody can take my pride, nobody can hold me down—oh no, I got to keep on moving, why? Because self-determination is no lie that's why! Puff-Daddy and I, will always agree—you see, we just can't let it be—both him and me, will keep singing, louder please! Nobody can take our pride, nobody can hold us down—oh no, we got to keep on moving. Shit sounds sweet to me! How about you black America? So raise your fists in the air, and wave em high like you just don't care and sing. Nobody can what? ✸

☼Word up black-ass dope dealers, stop the genocidal violence my sisters and brothers—mark your drugs <u>for white's only</u>! Refuse to sell your poison to black addicts! Besides, whites can pay a higher price for dope—since they steal more and kill more than dope itself—believe it! ✸

☼Most Honorable Malcolm X—please hurry back to those of us you left behind blind! Truly, God never meant for African kings to be monogamous—"because one cow is never enough! A true king deserves a whole herd of heifers!" <u>His story</u> is not our history! ✸

☼Nothing burns my ass up more then hearing (like niggers were saying back in the thirties and forties) black people today saying shit like "*I'm giving, spending, investing my monies with <u>white folks</u>, they got class, smarts, the right stuff, or attitudes—to win, succeed and achieve*" (and quick to kill). Talk about self-deprecating, race-destructive bullshit! How do we come to still believe such nonsense in this day and age. Some black folks will never learn—whenever we give our money, love, or intelligence to white America, she will find a way to slap us in our faces, to remind us of our places every time! When America gives thousands of dollars to Japanese survivors of W.W. II internment camps, then turns around and suggest to black Americans that slavery and its many negative after effects on and inside black people, doesn't rate consideration of any reparations (not even affirmative assistance) from our government—is the greatest slap in the faces of any single group of people ever, in the entire history of America!—Believe it! Reparations are way past due! Where is our 40 acres and mule? Bet'cha Ward Connelly knows. ✸

☼Yoh—Mr. Roger Moore, guess how many black sympathizers you have in Flint and Detroit, Michigan? So many you couldn't count them all, you go white boy. ✸

☼An International Question: is Mr. Nelson Mandela truly President of South Africa and truly free? I understand them white folks over there still desire to form their own separate government again—after 280 years of white rule and deadly racist apartheid. My people—please don't allow Affirmative Action to die out, get out and vote! Mandela did—you can too! ✸

☼History Lesson #1—The term Pic-Nic—Let's see, it's a summer weekend in the old south, so pick a nigger, hang him high, castrate him, set his body on fire—bring a basket of food and your kids, for a fun time—Sat., July 4th, 1920. Long live the spirit of brothers Huey Newton Eldridge Clever and sister Angela Davis. We have the right to defend ourselves! ✸

☼History Lesson #2—My brothers and sisters, music lovers, remember those Beatles—those white boys from England and their famous song—I Want To Hold Your Hand?... . Well did you know that Mr. Billy Preston was called the Fifth-Beatle? So titled by them out of gratitude, for holding their hands (teaching them rhythm and blues techniques) at their beginnings. Behind every great white-band (group) in the world, is that soulful black influence! Let us pray for Brother Preston's addiction, before he succumbs to it. Blacks do not import drugs into America-period! The enemies of black people do—everyday. ✸

☼Maya Angelou and Terry McMillian—you go girls, keep it up! Write that good shit! ✸

☼To all you black (new-age) health freaks out there. Could you, would you, cut those less health conscious brothers and sisters of yours a little more slack! So what if they like to occasionally sip a little cognac, and smoke them a pack. Truly the only life they're threatening is their own! So all you health-nuts should truly be grateful that they're not sipping on some Cisco (cheap rot-gut-wine) or Wild Irish Rose, and smoking Crack, because then your life would be really threatened whenever you didn't keep your dry-ass humor and sarcasm to yourselves! A young health freak recently jumped into my Jeep chariot and exclaimed, damn Big Earl, I smell cigarette smoke, I then said damn, young lady, I smell tuna fish. She asked if she could then get out, and I said no, because I love tuna fish. She smiled as I gently slipped my hand between her knees. Yes, she was wearing pants. ✸

☼Honorable Dr. Martin Luther King, Jr., we miss you so much—Yeah we do! Still, not all states in America honor your birthday—damn, just another slap on black America's cheek! ✸

LAST TWO PAGES—UNCHAINED

☼I don't know about you black America, but I am extremely hesitant to shake hands with White people now-a-days. Why is this so? Well honestly, truthfully, sincerely, over the last 25 years of my adult professional life. I have witnessed thousands of so-called educated, professional white men enter the bathrooms of America, use them, flush, then leave out, without washing their damn hands! You wonder just how civilized they really are. If you don't believe what I've just said, just observe your white co-workers or friends for a while. Shaking unwashed hands can be extremely hazardous to your health. Remember I told you so. ✸

☼Generally speaking—there are three different types of <u>black people</u> living in America at present. #1, those who truly don't know that they're black #2, and those who truly don't want to be black and #3, those five or six million who are always black and proud of it. They're the ones amongst the rest of us who are pro-active in continuing the struggle, for the freedom and equality of us all! (i.e., black Christian Nationalist) They shall be counted among the last survivors of our race. Question: Any of us seen a real red-man (American Indian) around town or the city, lately? I didn't think so. Lord have mercy! Especially on group #2 above—the real living Willie Lynch victims! Their parents didn't teach them shit about black history in America—not a damn thing! ✸

☼$1,000,000 donated to the Hon. Minister Louis Farrakan scares the hell out of white folks, but, $123,000,000 for a black high school basketball player does not. I think white folks dun-gon-crazy—- or have they? I don't think so! They got the National Guard, the banks, the heart (the balls!) and courage to defend their existence and way of life. Why not us? ✸

☼If just one more elite, bourgeois, conservative nigger—gets in my face one more time about not being so sensitive to racist-remarks, or the N-word, so that "it"—racism and hate crimes against black people can be allowed to fade away, I'm going to catch me a case over this fool and his ignorance. Bet! Ignorance is truly dangerous! Especially among ignorant whites with guns! ✸

☼What's up black men—wannabe men—are any of you besides me, listening to Bishop T.D. Jakes when he ask—all *of us, "What has happened to our generation? When we were little boys, we were afraid to walk into crowds of men—now we men are afraid to walk into crowds of little boys."* Black men must stay strong, fearless, and proud in any crowd. Especially amongst young black males and we know this! It takes strong black men to raise strong black males... period! ✸

☼Over heard recently in a women's washroom by one of my true sisters—dig! *"Girl you know black men don't listen, they don't read, and they have no memories of the shit they've told you the day before! Yeah girl, and they really don't gossip like we do—they just flat out lie?"* These ladies are obviously used to dealing with little boys—who have yet to become real men. My sister—which wash room was that, and where can I find these misguided gossiping little girls! ✸

☼A great civil-rights fighter and true friend of black folks has passed on. The late Father William T. Cunningham, 1930—1997 of Detroit, Michigan—the co-founder of Focus Hope, Inc.—rest in peace and God's loving grace Father, because you've earned it! We will always remember your selfless help, your strength and humor, and your precious and fearless stance on issues of civil rights (through out the 80's-90's) here in Detroit. Again, thank you for your fight against racial injustice and that good-ass Focus Hope cheese, that made the best cheese-toast, and my Moma's home-made macaroni and cheese! God bless you Mr. Cunningham. 4-Real Doe! ✸

☼Ok—Ok, so I missed his majesty the Pope and Mr. Billy Clinton—next time I won't! Between the two of them, it's any wonder in this country and around the world racial and tribal genocide continues to exist—Damn it, just wait! ✸

☼Shouts out to two beautiful black kids on the righteous path—Letitia and Edward K., Love Dad. All black kids are beautiful to me. ✸

☼Black power to all black people—never swap your guns for cheese!—Never! You may need them most, when you least expect it. Never surrender them! Never sell out! ✸

☼Oh yes—one more thing. All you dark-skinned Negroes wearing those bleached blond hair styles, it looks like shit! (even on Dennis Rodman)—so stop it, please—stop it! Get some black pride, or go home and stay inside. Blacks with bright blond or artificial white hair need to learn how to hide. Hah! I'm reaching for my glock. (Hint)—a black Barbie doll is still a white Barbie doll—only with a tan. You hair-wars people ought to check yourself, before you wreck yourself (and other blacks)! Black people's hair is a living thing—so let it live as it was born to do! Remember, nappie is nice! Christ wasn't' ashamed of his sheep's wool! ✸

☼Thank you oh Universal God—and you too mother/father for your gifts of life and love and also Gladys, Pam, Bonita, and Lue. Sister Sarah eat your heart out, you too Dan!✸

☼Peace and love to all my true black brothers and sisters who struggle onward and upward. Stay pro-active and keep reading, until we meet again and we will! Keep watching your backs and those so-called white friends. Black friends are predictable and usually controllable ✸

☼To the progeny of the "last poets"—go head rap masters, rap on my brothers and sisters, America is Listening! To all black African-Americans , better be ready for martial law, contrary to popular belief—white folks are not invincible! But are destructive and united! Bet and true that! If blacks ever again get out of hand—watch out! We just might gain even more respect! ✸

☼God bless and have mercy on a local-young-black radical artist T.G… "the polka-dot man! Your rights to the freedom of artistic expression is protected under the constitution of these United States of America! Ooops! Sorry brother, you're black, your art controversial, and misunderstood by your own people—so your rights as an American—well –truthfully—it's a damn toss-up! Fuck it! Let's take it to the white house!. ✸

☼A black associate brother of mine, recently told me he and his "church" didn't celebrate Martin Luther King's birthday, but did celebrate Labor Day, President's Day, Christmas and Independence Day. When I asked him why not? He said " his white pastor told him it was their church's tradition not to do anything special, just to hold regular services as usual." Question to my people—- was this pastor being sincere and honest? Or was he the wolf in sheep's clothing preparing to lead his flock of sheep to the slaughter. (Remember Rev. Jim Jones of Guyana?) Black people need to be careful where they tithe. They could be financing their own spiritual destruction—damn the blind—- bet! ✱

To those of you who've read this book and think that I'm out of my mind, do me a favor! Pop that coochie and back that thang up! In other words, fuck what you heard!! The white controlled media will continue to tell us that we are less than they, those with blond hair and bluest eyes! Don't fall victim to these subtle-racist, manipulative lies! Believe only what your heart and soul tells you. We were once a great and mighty race -- a proud people too! We will be that way again one day - oh yes, its true. If we collectively believe it, we will collectively achieve it! Black Americans must lead the way. So go tell it, tell someone half black (mentally) you got the word... "black is still beautiful - fuck what they heard!" Everybody black is entitled to a little light (true knowledge of self) under the sun, under the sun, under the sun......

LAST PAGE—FOR NOW

✡What Martin Luther King knew, and tried ceaselessly to communicate to America, was that a man who is not free inside himself cannot understand freedom. Any man who does not fully value and find meaning in his own life cannot feel the worth of all other individual lives. Martin Luther King also knew that words alone were not enough. That the preaching of redemptive love was not enough. He spoke truth to black people too! "*when a people are mired in oppression, they realize deliverance only when they have accumulated the power to enforce change. The troublesome task for negroes today (as of 1965) is to discover how to organize their strength into compelling power so that government cannot elude our demands. We must develop, from strength. Our strength comes from our being united,*" and yet—35 years later, in America our goals are still the same! True freedom and real equality for all black people, maybe 35 years from now or maybe 135 years from the day this page was written—Nov. 27, 1998—Thanksgiving Day! I hope not, that long, lost hope is not an option.✸

✡Message to my people (black folks) the readers of this book, I have given of my soul the words contained herein—if you are pleased, I am glad. If you are not—it doesn't matter. Just remember, the Tom-Tom cries and the Tom-Tom laughs. Guess which one I'm doing right now! Please excuse some of my tears on some of the pages. I have nothing but love and respect for all my people—believe it. I'm also stock piling canned goods, water, and ammo in my basement—our mutual struggle is not over by far, just wait till white folks here about this book! I know some negro gon-run-and-tell, Masser, Masser, there's a new black militant on the block in the hood! No I'm not new to the hood, and I'm not alone, but I'm proud to be called a black anything—Just don't call me boy or nigger! Peace out! It's been a ball—ya'll... B.B.E.R.✸

AN ACKNOWLEDGEMENT
TUNK—THANK YOU

Anybody for some tunk? Shouts out to all those brothers and sisters who believed in me—Thank you! Dream bigger dreams. Come back to black. It's beautiful and indestructible-truly!

Hey ya'll! Set out some of that hot cat-fish please (to all those player-haters who didn't believe in me) -Thank you, too! Better get a dream! Study your history to believe in yourself!

There just better be some hot-sauce around here! To all those brothers and sisters who believed in themselves and our continual struggle here in America. Thank you for staying the course. The meek shall inherit the earth.

Quick—somebody turn up Marvin Gaye—Got to give it up! To all those Player-Haters who have never believed in themselves—shame on you—go get a life and live it! God, I miss Marvin Gaye, damn! Even today, some black fathers don't play! Just like me. Thanks mom and dad and (my big sister) for instilling in me self pride and the courage to tell the truth.

Tunk, I win! Anybody for some strip-poker? OK, but please put the kids to bed first
They don't need to see what comes next... Stay tuned for Big Earl's second book "Big Earl Speaks—Book II—Keeping Shit Real". Peace out! Raising the urban roof collectively!

Oh hell yeah!... and to all those other folks who helped turn this book into a reality, be proud of your blackness—never give up—never sell out. The struggle is not yet over! Between the years of 1882 to 1927, over 3,500 black people were known to have been lynched! In 1998, a black man was tied to the back of a truck by three white men and dragged over three and a half miles to his death in Jasper Texas, for the crime of being black in America and in the wrong place at the wrong time! How many blacks have been murdered since 1927 to the present, by whites for similar reasons? Integration has proved deadly for black Americans. So God bless you all—I'll take my chances with my AK-47! So I beg your damn pardon—was it something I said? Oh yeah? Well, fuck it, I feel better and I told the truth! Case closed, I'm out of here—F.O.I. until I die! Long live our black genes!

Protect us God! For we black folks are still unwilling and apparently unable to protect (defend) ourselves! Far too many of us still equate success and survival with cowardice, kissing white and black asses to get ahead, daily abusing and stabbing our own black people in the back - just to gain a promotion or fucking fancy title and wear Rolex watch! Stand with us Lord, for blacks in America still have long road to travel. Real equality and justice still require courage and sacrifice, and we know this! Even today - it seems we still don't have the common sense or guts to do it for ourselves! "Say what Lord?" - Call Mike Tyson, a true black warrior? Yeah! That's cool! Maybe one day I'll see one black nation under a groove, collectively getting down for the funk of it, maybe - one day - Amen.

Big Brother Earl Roberts

www.ingramcontent.com/pod-product-compliance
Ingram Content Group UK Ltd.
Pitfield, Milton Keynes, MK11 3LW, UK
UKHW041943190726
13854UKWH00004B/1767